Endors

"Most of us live our lives outside in, overly influenced by the world around us. Abe Daniel shows us how to live inside out, by faith."

—Mark Batterson
New York Times bestselling author of
The Circle Maker

"Abe Daniel is the real deal. He has found a way to translate his life-transforming tragedy on a golf course, and—with God's help—turn it into an insightful lesson for each of us. For most of us, this accident would have been puzzling: why would God allow it? But Abe's puzzle became a pulpit. I encourage you to listen to his message."

—Dr. Tim Elmore
Best-selling author of *Habitudes*,
founder of GrowingLeaders.com

"I love it when an author combines their life experiences with Biblical truths to provide encouragement to their readers. FORE! will take you on a journey to starve your doubt and feed your faith."

—Rev. Doug Clay
General Superintendent, Assemblies of God USA

"This book is a faith builder with solid biblical perspective on suffering and healing. Pastor Abe's personal story makes it real and reachable for anyone that needs to be inspired to believe God is still doing miracles."

—Dr. Frank Damazio
Chairman, Ministers Fellowship International
Author of *The Making of a Leader*

"A golfer, I am not. A person who has walked through dark valleys where unexpected suffering has slammed against my life, I am. In FORE! Finding Faith When You're Paralyzed by Your Circumstances, Pastor Abe Daniel tells his own riveting story of what it means to experience both physical and spiritual paralysis. Through the trauma of what most would call a freak accident, Abe encountered his faithful God in new ways. Written with equal parts humor and raw honesty, and woven together with rich biblical truths, Pastor Abe's painful, miraculous journey has become a well-marked path towards divine promise for the rest of us. If you'll pardon the pun (sorry, not sorry), don't miss this 'hole in one' of hope!"

—Dr. Jodi Detrick
Author of *The Jesus-Hearted Woman,* and
*The Settled Soul: Tenaciously Abiding
with a Tender God*

"My dear friend Pastor Abe Daniel has allowed God to use and teach him through what can only be described as a crisis. He tells his story in ways no one else can, and you don't have to be a golf fan to appreciate the heart and nuance of this book. In FORE!, Abe will take you through the course of his life and encourage you in whatever stage of faith you find yourself."

—Rev. Samuel Rodriguez
New Season-Lead Pastor
NHCLC President/CEO
Author *Persevere With Power; What Heaven Starts,
Hell Cannot Stop!*
Exec. Producer *Breakthrough* and
Flamin Hot Movies

"One of the greatest gifts we can give to others is courage in every season. Abe Daniel has written a book that does just that. FORE! is the story of God's goodness in the midst of difficult circumstances. I believe it will lead you to a deeper place of faith and greater courage we so desperately need."

—Banning Liebscher
Jesus Culture Founder and Pastor

"Everyone has a story. Everyone has a journey they've traveled, which has shaped who they are. Author Abe Daniel is no different. In his book, FORE!, he chronicles his riveting story filled with challenges and victories. With humor and depth, he reveals life principles and spiritual truths that will guide you on your own journey. When authors request an endorsement for their respective book, I ask myself three questions: Does the author have something to say? Does the author possess the right motives? And, does the author honor Jesus by how he or she lives? Abe Daniel and FORE! check all three boxes. From cover to cover, this book will be a blessing to your life."

—Hal Donaldson
Founder/CEO, Convoy of Hope

"Pastor Abe Daniel does a masterful job of taking you through a journey of his own personal pain and difficulty to bring fresh and relevant perspective to timeless biblical principles. FORE! is filled with wisdom, humor, wit and biblical application that is absolutely essential for every Christian person to know, understand and practice in the reality of today's world."

—Rev. Bret Allen
District Superintendent, Assemblies of God
Northern California & Nevada
Author of *Lead, Follow, or Get Out of the Way* and
Shift! Are you relevant or just recent?

"Valley seasons are part of everyone's story. And while we'd never choose them, this book provides a framework for leveraging them but not living in them. In FORE!, Abe points us to a powerful perspective that comes from personal experience. His humor, candor, and practical insights will assist anyone desiring to make the most of every moment."

—Dr. Jeffery Portmann
Director - Church Multiplication Network USA

"Rev. Abe Daniel is my friend. I've watched his life for decades. His story will motivate, inspire, challenge, and encourage you on your journey of faith, especially in those difficult patches. You'll want to share this book with others. It's more than a story, it's a testimony of perseverance, a wife's love and God's amazing grace."

—Dr. Samuel M. Huddleston
Assistant District Superintendent, Assemblies of God
Northern California & Nevada
Author of *Five Years to Life* and *Grand Slam*

FORE!

FINDING FAITH WHEN YOU'RE PARALYZED BY YOUR CIRCUMSTANCES

ABE DANIEL

FREILING
PUBLISHING

Bible versions used:

The Holy Bible, English Standard Version. ESV® Text Edition: 2016.
Copyright © 2001 by Crossway Bibles, a publishing ministry of
Good News Publishers.

Holy Bible, New International Version®, NIV® Copyright ©1973,
1978, 1984, 2011 by Biblica, Inc.® Used by permission.
All rights reserved worldwide.

The New King James Version® (NKJV). Copyright © 1982
by Thomas Nelson. Used by permission. All rights reserved.

The Message (MSG). Copyright © 1993, 2002, 2018
by Eugene H. Peterson

Published by Freiling Publishing, a division of Freiling Agency, LLC.

P.O. Box 1264
Warrenton, VA 20188

www.FreilingPublishing.com

PB ISBN: 978-1-956267-54-9
eBook ISBN: 978-1-956267-55-6

Printed in the United States of America

Dedication

This book is dedicated to my loving and supportive wife, Anna! It was during this season that I write about that you stood by me when I was unable to physically stand. It was during this very crisis I write about that I saw and experienced your love before we publicly declared these vows to the world … for better, for worse, for richer, for poorer, in sickness and in health, to love and to cherish. Thank you for the way that you still stand with and support me. Thank you for the way that you model true love, grace, and strength in our family and all those you serve. I truly love you!

Table of Contents

Foreword

I think a lot about hope. In fact, you could say it is the most defining word in my life. I run a nonprofit organization called OneHope, where our mission is to bring the hope that can only be found in God and His Word to every child on Earth. I also co-authored a best-selling book on changing your world with hope as a central value. Even my favorite quote from St. Augustine is all about hope, "Hope has two beautiful daughters: their names are Anger and Courage. Anger at the way things are, and Courage to see that they do not remain as they are."

What happens, as I've certainly experienced, when no amount of anger, courage, or even faith will seemingly change the reality of the present situation? This is a question Abe Daniel was forced to seek an answer to during the darkest moment in his life, and a question I've often wrestled with myself.

As you'll soon find out through this book, Abe has experienced a crisis that left him in emotional, physical, and spiritual turmoil. He knows what it's like to feel no relief in the midst of pain–to feel hopeless. His faith was challenged, but through it, he learned about the stages we all go through when our faith feels like it's dwindling, and his words are an encouragement to any who find themselves in a similar spot.

I met Abe for the first time when I was a fresh college graduate. I had just gotten married and began serving as a youth pastor at Abe's church. Even though he was only 10 years old, Abe had a burning love for God and a passion for ministry. His hunger for more of Jesus was so great that my wife and I decided he should join the youth ministry. He ended up serving in worship and leading our church family even after we left.

I've had the honor to watch that little boy grow into a man of God for more than 35 years, and though I still remember the pain of seeing him go through the accident, it is so beautiful to see the depth of vulnerability, courage, and wit throughout his story.

This book has been such a crucial reminder in my own life that hope can be found in the darkness. I've recently had people I deeply care about face menacing and imminent evil in the midst of war and I've sat with my stepmom as she battles an aggressive cancer that has her in constant pain. No amount of vitriol on my part could change those realities. War and cancer rage on, and I am powerless to stop either.

So what are we to do when no amount of science, theology, or experience can fix the reality of orphans trapped in a bomb shelter in enemy territory or a loved one whose insides are chemically on fire? No amount of money or missional strategy can stop a war, and no doctor or pain med can relieve the agony cancer causes. All the hope verses that I have memorized feel empty today.

However, herein lies the ultimate paradox of Kingdom citizens: we live fully in the present and fully in the future. We operate fully in the seen and unseen realms. We take on the incarnational nature of our King, who decided as God to come and live and operate in the temporal, painful, finite world. We live in this present age, but our citizenship transcends it.

Abe's story is an incredible reminder that when I feel an absence of faith and hope in the midst of my present situation, I am asked to live in the certainty of future hope. Abe allows us to accompany him on his own journey to finding true faith and joy in the Lord, no matter the pain and hopelessness he experienced along the way.

Throughout his story, I have found a respite, relief, a reminder of what is waiting, perhaps through healing in the here and now, but a certainty, a hope against hope, that we as His children are destined for eternal joy and peace in Him. I am confident that this book will do the same for you.

—Dr. Rob Hoskins
President, OneHope
Best-selling author of *Change Your World: How Anyone, Anywhere Can Make a Difference*

Introduction

Faith is a word that sparks great strength or the potential of fear in my life! The strength is found when I remain grounded in my trust in God. The fear is discovered when my extreme circumstances of life overshadow my ability to see Him as my strength. Faith is something that should be at the foundation of our life as Christians, and yet, I find that it is something that I frequently battle. It is in the personal battles that I have encountered along my journey that have translated into true faith defining moments.

I believe that most understand the concept of a defining moment. A defining moment is described as, *"a point at which the essential nature or character of a person, group, etc., is revealed or identified."*[1] History is filled with defining moments. My enjoyment of studying history began in High School and has increased ever since. As I have continued to study, I have realized that each decade contains defining moments within our nation's history. In the 1960s, the assassination of President Kennedy and the Apollo 11 Moon landing became defining moments within that decade. If we fast forward into the early 2000s, we still remember the September 11, 2001, attacks upon our nation. Each of these events and the many in between both shaped and even pointed our nation in a new direction.

I believe that the same is true for our lives as well. Defining moments for an individual can occur when we begin a new job, or a romantic relationship. In these cases, they can continue to grow as the job leads to a career, or that relationship leads to marriage. While sometimes we don't recognize the moment to be significant, at some point, we are able to trace back these milestones to defining moments.

While there is a natural side to this, we see the spiritual impact as Christ-followers. Our defining moments begin when we accept Christ as our Lord and Savior. They continue as we discover His plan and purpose for our lives. They increase as we realize that the trials and crisis moments we face, are to prepare us for the things He has next.

The major trauma that I encountered that is highlighted in this book, revealed four stages in which my faith was challenged. At each identified stage, we are given the chance to stand and fight, or sit and in many cases, slowly perish. My prayer is that this book can encourage you along your faith journey! My prayer is that you will not look at the difficult situation you find yourself in and become paralyzed by your circumstances. My prayer is that you allow this book to be a support to you as you are in the middle of a faith building defining moment.

I pray that my journey and some of the life lessons of faith can provide you the grace and strength you need for the days ahead. While you will soon discover that this book has a golf theme, my prayer is that you can see me as one who has gone slightly ahead on this "faith course" and yell back "FORE!" to prepare you for the potential of impact.

Abe Daniel

STAGE 1

Beware

"Golf is a fascinating game. It has taken me nearly
40 years to discover that I can't play it.[2]"
—Ted Ray

I love golf but don't know if I qualify to be called a
"golfer." To be considered a "golfer," you have to
effectively "play" this game, which includes precision,
endurance, and a strong eye. I don't know that any
of my friends who have endured a round of golf with
me would say that I "play" this game. Regardless, it
is a game that I enjoy. It takes forever to complete a
round, is very costly, requires expensive equipment,
the clothing is odd, watching it on TV is boring to
many, and yet, I love it all. What I did not know was
that this amazing sport would be connected to me for
the rest of my life based on a crisis.

Consistently playing this game since the age of
eighteen has taught me a lot related to this sport. My
first round, however, was at the age of twelve with my
dad, a family friend, and a childhood friend. On that
day, the two twelve-year-old kids crashed the rented
golf cart by driving through a large sand trap. Because
I was in trouble, I don't count that as when I began

playing. It would be ten years later, on that exact same hole that I would have another golf cart accident that would truly change my life.

As I started learning this sport, I was introduced to the language and terminology associated with golf. There were so many words that I truly did not understand while beginning. There were words like "par," "birdie," "bogie," "double bogie," "triple bogie," and many more. I was also introduced to a four-letter word that I was allowed to speak while playing golf. Now, before you begin to fill in the blank prematurely, the word and most-used phrase I have learned is the expression "FORE!" "FORE!" is what I shout when I'm in jeopardy of hitting a ball toward a person or group in front of me.

According to Scottish golf history dating back to the early 1800s, there are multiple originations of this powerful word. One of which is associated with what is known as a *Forecaddie*. "Because golf balls were expensive, golfers employed 'Forecaddies' to stand where the ball might land and reduce the number of lost balls, as is done in tournaments today. It is probable that golfers shouted to their 'Forecaddie!', who would always be some distance ahead to draw attention to the fact the ball was coming, and, in time, this was shortened to 'Fore!' The almost contemporaneous appearance of the terms caddie, fore-caddie, and 'Fore!' supports this theory over the others."[3]

Now if you are not a golfer, you've already tuned out. The reality of this book is not to give you the history of golf, but rather to challenge the reader how to respond with the unforeseen obstacles that are coming your way. John 16:33 says, *"I have said these things to you, that in me you may have peace. In the world you will have tribulation. But take heart; I have overcome the world."*[4]

The phrase "...you will have tribulation..." is guaranteed to overwhelm us. The word "tribulation" is not an everyday word we hear in conversations. Outside of a church service, I don't think that the word tribulation is one that I use as I'm going about my daily life. The Message version of scripture translates that phrase to *"you will continue to experience difficulties..."*[5] One of the most depressing realizations anyone—especially a Christian—can have is that we are guaranteed tribulation or difficulties.

The Apostle John wrote about this summary and climax of the Upper Room message. It was a preparation moment for each of the disciples from Jesus Himself because He knew that these men and the generations that reach down to us would experience tribulations, difficulties, and severe trials. One commentary I read on this passage stated that there is a vast difference between the phrases within this passage. There is a difference between the words "in me" and "in the world." In Christ, there is peace. In this world, there is a guarantee of tribulation. The position that we need to claim is that because we are in Christ, we are overcomers![6]

As a pastor, I have many conversations with people surrounding the theme of faith. Many new Christ followers have an assumption that serving Christ is a guaranteed protection that nothing bad will ever happen to them. One of the hardest revelations that we have at some point in our walk of faith is that we are not exempt from trials just because we are Christians. Our guarantee is found in Psalm 23:4 which says, *"Even though I walk through the valley of the shadow of death, I will fear no evil, for you are with me; your rod and your staff, they comfort me."[7]*

> The guarantee of life's valleys is overwhelming but possible to move beyond because He, my Heavenly Father, the Creator of the Universe, is with me.

I believe that the 23rd Psalm is one of the most famous passages in scripture, if not the most famous of them all. I have heard it read countless times at funerals as a way of offering comfort to a grieving family. Christians and even non-Christians have the possibility of being able to recite portions—if not all of it. However, I have realized that many, including myself, have never truly understood these words that are found in verse four until we experience a crisis. The more I have studied this verse, the more I notice this guarantee that I will go through a valley. The guarantee of life's valleys is overwhelming but possible to move beyond because He, my Heavenly Father, the Creator of the Universe, is with me.

One of the things that causes us greater issues in navigating the valleys of our lives is the surprise factor. Most of the crisis moments, issues, or tribulation moments that I have encountered have caught me at a time when I wasn't expecting it. It's equivalent to hearing someone yell "FORE!" and then being hit by a ball. There isn't enough time to react. There isn't any place to move. By the time you hear it, it's too late.

There is a guarantee that each of us will have to navigate the valleys of life. Based on the valleys I have navigated, I have a desire to yell "FORE!" as a warning of what is ahead. This is not to live our lives with a spirit of fear. But rather, to live ready to respond to what is ahead as opposed to reacting too late. This posture would have served me better when my crisis began.

> This is not to live our lives with a spirit of fear. But rather, to live ready to respond to what is ahead as opposed to reacting too late.

Again, the idea of being ready for a crisis is not something you can adequately prepare for. If I had been ready, my outcome would not have changed, but I would have arrived sooner and been healthy through the journey.

HOLE #1

Upon personal reflection, I don't think I had experienced a true crisis within my life until my early twenties and for that I am blessed and truly grateful. In June of 1998, I felt as if I was on top of the world. If you had met and asked me during that time, I would have probably said that a trial or even crisis was not possible for me. I had just finished college and had been hired as a full-time Associate Pastor (a part-time position that I had held for four years prior). This was what I saw as the beginning of all that God had spoken to me as a twelve-year-old child called into ministry. The idea that a church would pay me to do something that I had volunteered for blew my mind and caused me a greater sense of security and possible denial to the vulnerability of what was coming.

During this season, I was dating for a three-year period the one and only girl I've ever dated. Anna and I met during our college years, and I knew this is who I wanted to spend the rest of my life with. Knowing this, I went to my parents first and received their blessing to propose marriage. Everything felt as if it was perfectly lined up. My personal life was progressing, my future marital life was taking shape and I may have felt invincible.

One of the greatest joys was not only the idea of marriage and beginning my first full-time ministry position, but it was also connected to the amazing relationships that I had built in ministry. Proverbs 17:17 says, *"A friend loves at all times, and a brother is born for adversity."* [8] I was blessed to have these kinds of friends in my life. Again, I reflected upon a content season of my life. I had a loving and supportive family, a future with my soon-to-be fiancé, the arrival into full-time ministry and continued pursuit of my pastoral calling and friends I liked! Nothing could have made that moment better.

Monday, June 8, 1998, began as a normal day. I had received a request to drive my pastor and his wife to the airport as they were heading on vacation to celebrate their wedding anniversary. My pastor was navigating his own series of crisis moments as he was battling leukemia during this season. Their ability to escape for a few days of vacation was rare and made it that much more special. As I reflect today, I still remember his words to me as I dropped them off at the airport. He said what many pastors have said to their team members before leaving on vacation, "Don't call unless someone dies!" The thought of that statement all these years later still makes me smile. While I was driving back to my office, I received a call from a true friend. This is the kind of friend that others hope to have and keep as we all navigate this earthly journey. Tony Orlando (not the singer) is one of those friends that I still have in my life decades later. Tony's call stated that a group of friends were going to play a round of golf that evening and wondered if I wanted to join them. The thought of enjoying golf with friends was (and still is) always welcomed. After accepting, I realized that I now had a schedule conflict. I had a leadership meeting scheduled with students that evening. My brain works hard to process problems very fast, and I immediately started to work this small detail out. Since I had played this very short golf course weekly for years, I knew that I could play and be done within one hour. I quickly agreed to join them and met everyone around 5 p.m. that evening.

I was not only excited to play, but I was also excited to head home to change into my golf outfit. Though it was several hours away, I knew that this was the best usage of my time... to dress for the occasion. I had just purchased a new visor (something I had never worn in my life) and thought it would at least give the appearance of proficiency with golf. I have always golfed with the mindset, if you can't play well, you should at least look as if you play well. I don't know if this was a good choice, but it would also become the last day I would ever wear a visor.

There was a great reunion of friends as we all arrived in the parking lot that evening. While we were reconnecting, I was also being introduced to others that I had never met. Our group consisted of pastors, church members, family members, and friends of friends. As we were checking in and paying our fees, we began to realize that our initial group had grown beyond just a few of us. The average golf group pairing is four golfers, and we now had a total of eight golfers broken into two groups. I knew that this would cause us to play slower and thought it would be wise to rent a golf cart. Knowing that I would most likely need to leave early, my two friends agreed that we would split a cart between the three of us and ride together. Though golf carts are intended for two riders, the bench seat makes it possible to cram three if needed. We were grateful that the golf pro at the front desk was willing to collect money from all three of us towards the rental of the golf cart so that we could begin. As we headed out to the first tee box, we were truly enjoying each other's presence, but quietly, I was incredibly nervous due to the extreme competitive nature that I had (and may still have).

I was part of group one and was the last to tee off. With the first hole being less than 100 yards, you would naturally assume that this would be easy and fairly quick. The first three golfers in our group teed off and did well landing around—and even on—the green. I, however, did not do as well and hit the ball right (which I still do to this day). As the ball went distinctly right, it crossed the fence, landing in the field next to the course. Most would think that hitting your first shot out of bounds, receiving a penalty, and potentially losing a ball would be very bad. My shot went from bad to worse as I did not just hit it out of bounds, I also hit a cow. This is not a metaphor; my shot actually struck a cow. I'm still uncertain if this would have been an appropriate time to yell "FORE?" Regardless, this should have been my indication that this day was not going to end well!

I don't know if I even realized what had happened or if it was well known that I had hit the cow. I feel that if it was, I would have had a much harder time saving face in that moment. Being cheap or as I like to call, "financially wise", I decided to jump the fence to see if I could find my ball. After a little bit of searching, I hit my ball (or one that was similar to what I had previously hit) back into play and finished the hole with a wonderful seven. In case you don't know, golf is a sport where the player strives to achieve the lowest number of strokes possible per hole. On this par three hole (where the average golfer should complete it in three strokes or less), I more than doubled the average by recording a seven. This was not the greatest way to begin but it caused me to be more determined to fix what I had obviously started.

HOLE #2

I walked to the second tee box frustrated, but ready to redeem myself. I again was last to hit due to the fact that I had done so poorly on the first hole. I don't remember much of the conversations that were happening around me due to my personal embarrassment. What I do remember was what happened when it was my turn to hit again. As I was stepping up to set my ball down, one of the seven golfers, a part of our other group shouted, "You may have a greater chance to hit the hole if we move that cow over to the green!" Again, I have amazing friends. As I approached the ball, I was now hitting it with anger, embarrassment, frustration, and still my competitive nature. I will now confess that I was also picturing the face of the "friend" on the ball that I was about to hit because he shouted the smart comment of moving the cow to this hole. I have heard over the years that there are between seven to twenty different things a golfer needs to remember to execute a good or even a great golf shot. There are days that I have remembered a few of them and others that I have accomplished the majority. On this day, at this moment, nothing else mattered except for hitting it as hard as I could. As I hit, the ball did something it had never done up until that moment and even to this day… it went straight, and it went far!

For the first time in my life, I hit a golf ball approximately 250 yards with a five-wood (not ideal for a hole that long and my size, but again, I wasn't thinking.) This particular shot went high in the air, crossed a large "gully" and landed in front of the green. It looked like a perfect golf shot until we realized that it wasn't done moving. It bounced and rolled another twenty yards stopping several feet away from the actual flag. I was shocked! My friends were shocked! The only thing that would have made this better is if the ball rolled the extra few feet into the hole, but again, I'm not a golfer! I turned to my friends who had all begun to cheer and announced, "Today is the last day that I will ever play this game because I will never hit a shot like that again!" As I pointed out before, I felt that this season of my life was the best and now I was truly on top of the world.

As we climbed into our golf cart, one friend was driving, my friend, Tony, was sitting in the middle, and I was sitting on the passenger side of this bench seat. We began to head down a steep cart path and continued to accelerate our speed as we descended. Anytime a vehicle is traveling at a speed that feels unsafe, it is natural for the driver to apply the brakes. And the natural reaction of wanting to slow down is exactly what our driver attempted. Again, for those that do not know golf or the equipment, the difference between a traditional vehicle's brakes and golf cart brakes is an additional mechanism called a hill brake. The hill brake of a golf cart is located on the top portion of the actual brake. When a hill brake is applied, a golfer can park a cart on a steep incline or decline without fear of it rolling away. This is possible based upon the mechanism that locks all four wheels in place.

When our hill brake was applied to the fast speed of our golf cart's descent, all four of the wheels locked up causing the cart to begin to flip. A gentle tapping of the break would have resulted in us slowing down as we passed through this gully toward our next shot. But due to the locking of all wheels, the cart began to react to the speed, the path conditions, the incline, and our driver's reaction. This ultimately resulted in our cart beginning to flip upside down. As the cart flipped, our driver was ejected to the left, my friend, Tony, was ejected through the center (thankfully, there was no windshield) and I was ejected to the right. I believe everything would have been okay at that point if that's where the story ended. But this would be the appropriate moment where someone needed to yell

"FORE!" because awareness of what was coming would be required.

What happened next took place so fast that I can't say that I saw any of it coming. While I had been ejected to the right of the path, the golf cart that had flipped, landed on top of me. Again, I want to emphasize that up until that moment in time, I had felt as if I was on top of the world. Invincible. Secure. Confident based on everything that had led up to that point. In one moment, I was on top of the world and the next moment—I was under a golf cart.

It's amazing to realize how much can change in a person's life in the matter of seconds. As the seven golfers from our two groups approached, they were able to lift and move the cart off me and immediately began to stare. For those of you wondering—the posture I was lying in is not one that I would ever wish to experience again, or have anyone else encounter. I knew that I was in pain, and I felt as if my body was contorted, but I was unaware of the extent of my injuries. The friends surrounding me began to check to see if I was coherent. One reached down to see if I was responsive, and my friend Tony asked if I could feel him tapping on my leg. To my alarm—I could not, but I don't even remember replying. Everyone knew something was wrong—including me—but none of us would fully understand how serious it would be for another several hours.

One friend began to pray and another one dialed 9-1-1. As I laid on the ground in significant pain, I felt more embarrassed than concerned about my situation. One of the golfers in our group was an EMT who continued to communicate with me, comfort me, and prevent me from moving due to the potential worst-case medical scenarios. I don't believe I ever knew how bad things were until I recognized how many people were involved. Groups of first responders began to arrive including the Highway Patrol, the local Fire Department, local Police, EMT first responders in their ambulance, and others. As each group arrived, they all looked at me with the same expressions my friends had given me, one of shock and disbelief.

I had the privilege of meeting one of my first responders over a year later who described with vivid detail all that he encountered upon arriving. He described me as, "laying on the ground, fairly well contorted." That was not a new revelation. What he followed with, was as he described my "head resting on my chest." My friend, Tony, would describe it to me years later by saying "…your chin was touching your sternum and your eyes were pointing up." For those of you readers who don't have a background in medical studies, I will just let you know—this is not normal nor is it natural.

One of the most difficult onsite decisions that needed to be made was whether they should stretch me out into a normal position or leave me contorted due to the high-risk nature of a neck injury. At some point, the decision was made (at my urging) to stretch me out before placing me in the ambulance. As they began to move me, I began to hear the first of multiple directives from professionals that urged me not to move as they adjusted me. Thankfully, they were able to stabilize my neck with a brace, attach me to a stretcher, and carry me to the ambulance. Little did I know that I would not be transported in this ambulance, but instead, it would become my holding room.

HOLE #3

Again, I go back to the thoughts of defining moments. It's one thing to think about the historical moments, and another to process defining moments on a personal level. When they are personal in my life, I know that these life events along this journey can shape me, my outlook on life, my family, and in my case, my ministry as well. I knew this could become one of those moments, so I decided in the back of an ambulance to begin capturing as many of them in my memory as possible. I made a conscious decision to enjoy what would become a life-long story to share, but also a forever sermon illustration that I would be able to reference as a pastor. I began to joke with the first responders, my friends, and my new captive audience on the golf course. I wasn't thinking of a crisis, I was being a twenty-something-year-old version of me and making the best of that moment. However, the first moment that I started to understand that it could possibly be serious was the moment I heard the sounds of a helicopter in the distance preparing to land on the first hole.

It wasn't long after it had landed that I was loaded into the helicopter for what would become my first ever ride in one. My sadness was that I was on my back and would not be able to look out of the window and enjoy the ride I was preparing for. As we were ready to take off, the paramedic on board asked if there was anything I needed before we took off. I answered "yes" and then asked for my friend, Tony.

True friends are the ones you can trust with both the majors and minors of life. They are the ones who will stand with you when you are at your lowest moment, they are the ones that will cheer loudest during your greatest victories. I am grateful that I was surrounded by this kind of a friend in that very moment. As Tony approached the helicopter, I asked him to help me with a few things. The first thing that I needed him to do was to drive my car back to my church office and leave it there. He kindly agreed. The second thing I needed from him was to call Anna (my girlfriend and future fiancé/now wife.) I asked him to let her know what happened without making it sound too serious. In my mind, I would be checked out and released within a few hours. There would be no need to cause anyone any grief or concern for something that wasn't too serious. He said that he would take care of it. The final thing I needed was associated with my desire to still enjoy every moment if possible. To this day, I can't believe that I asked this of him and even better, I can't believe that he did it. For my final request... I asked him to "go grab my golf ball." I remember him leaning in and asking me, "What did you say?" And I gently repeated it again, "Tony, go get my golf ball, it's on the green." I believe that the paramedic was officially done with my "needs" and informed us that it was time to go. At that moment, the door was closed, and we gently began to lift off from the golf course. One of my favorite memories was watching my friend, Tony, stand there for a few seconds as the helicopter was ascending. My last view of the course that I had was of him sprinting toward the second green to pick up my golf ball. I am grateful for these amazing friendships that I have to this day and the fact that I still retain that golf ball as a special "souvenir" that is featured on a bookshelf in my office.

HOLE #4

When on a golf course, my natural reaction to hearing the word *"FORE!"* is no longer to take cover and beware. My natural reaction is to look around to see who is dodging the impact of a foreign object approaching them at significant speeds. The reason I no longer take cover is based upon the assumption that it was not intended for me. There are many warning and caution signs that surround our world today. Just this week, I have seen signs that road crews are working ahead, I've seen hazard lights because of accidents, I've seen caution signs about pets on properties or railroad crossings and so many more. In fact, because I am constantly surrounded by these kinds of signs, I have become immune to noticing them.

The purpose in finally capturing some of my journey in print form is to be an encouragement to readers navigating this kind of faith journey. 1 Peter 4:12 says, *"Beloved, do not be surprised at the fiery trial when it comes upon you to test you, as though something strange were happening to you."* I have historically never lived with the anticipation of the fiery trials that are coming my way. A part of me believes that to live like this would be to live a life that constantly sees the glass being half empty.

> Our hearts must be focused, not upon the trials that are coming our way, but the hope in Him who will both guard and guide us through this moment.

Our world today has a constant fixation on the glass half empty mindset. In many cases, they have taken that philosophy to greater levels. They see the glass as being half empty and now starting to leak. They see the glass that is half empty and believe it will never be full again. They see the glass that is half empty and have become offended that we are talking about the glass. They see the glass that is half empty and begin to argue if we should pray for it to be full or if we should pray for a new glass.

And in some extreme cases, they see the glass that is half empty, but they have that attitude that it doesn't matter because only the rich get to drink water. They see the glass that is half empty and they blame it as the fault of a political party. They see the glass that is half empty and become worried that the glass is going to break. I believe that you get the idea!

This cannot afford to be the attitude for Christ-followers! Our hearts must be focused, not upon the trials that are coming our way, but the hope in Him who will both guard and guide us through this moment. While there is something unknown coming our way, He is with us! This is the same promise that we stated earlier from Psalm 23. Regardless of the valley that we are navigating, we as Christ followers have a promise… we are never alone, He is with us.

On Monday, June 8, 1998, I began the day on the top of a mountain only to find myself heading toward a dark valley. I will admit that like most normal people, the journey towards a valley is not one that I would normally choose. But regardless of

> **Your valley moment whether past, present or future is not where you are sentenced to live.**

my choice to travel there, or the possible discovery that I am already in the middle of one, the valley journey has never been unavoidable. Though it has never been unavoidable, each valley has been rich with hidden treasure. It is in the valley that I have been reminded that God is still present. In fact, His very presence in the valley, regardless of what we see or even feel can become our ground of confidence. This can sound like an amazing reflection today, but hard to remember when we are navigating the terrain of the valley.

If I had the ability to go back to that moment as this helicopter was ascending, I would have wanted to be reminded of a powerful truth.

Every valley can become a school to teach me.
Every valley can become a school to train me.
Every valley can sometimes be used to break me
so that I have the ability to walk in
a new power and a new spirit.

Though that was my foundation, all of it would be lost and/or forgotten because of the chaos I was feeling in the middle of my very own crisis moment.

If you find yourself heading towards a valley moment, in the middle of a valley, or even attempting to escape the valley, I challenge you to hold on to this simple promise. 2 Corinthians 12:9 says, *"But he said to me, 'My grace is sufficient for you, for my power is made perfect in weakness.' Therefore I will boast all the more gladly of my weaknesses, so that the power of Christ may rest upon me. "*[10] Your valley moment whether past, present or future is not where you are sentenced to live. Your valley moment is just that… a moment. It is a place where God's grace can be revealed. It is a place where God's strength can be felt. It is the place where we feel weak, but where His power makes us strong.

STAGE 2

Unfair/Despair

> *"The only time my prayers are never answered*
> *is on the golf course."*[11]
> —Rev. Billy Graham

It is one thing to hear the scream "FORE!" and to be alerted of some unidentified flying object approaching from out of nowhere. If it misses you, it's luck. If you are struck, you are unlucky. I have never met individuals who have been "struck" and believed they deserved it. In fact, most of the people I have encountered in my first few decades of ministry would tell you they felt that their sudden loss, tragedy, or crisis was unfair and/or out of nowhere. A good percentage of them would say that their crisis led them into a season of despair.

The definition of the word "despair" is "loss of hope; hopelessness."[12] Quite literally, it means the absence of hope. I believe that anyone who experiences crisis moments has the potential of shifting from a state of shock towards a state of despair. It's a state in which we assume the worst and expect nothing less. It is in these settings that I have always worked hard to remind myself of scripture, but frankly, most of it seems fuzzy at best. As I was entering my valley moment of crisis and navigating the journey ahead, I would repeatedly be reminded of the life of Joseph out of the book of Genesis.

Though Joseph is one of my favorite biblical characters, I feel as if elements of his life journey came to me at different points, as opposed to all at once. In my eyes, the journey that Joseph endured was not only one that we could easily describe as unfair, but it should have led him to despair. My quick summary of Genesis 37-39 includes: a favorite son being identified, favor, dreams, jealousy, revenge, slavery, favor again, temptation, accusation, false imprisonment, favor yet again, forgotten, and probably a lot more.

If I had taken the journey Joseph had to navigate, I believe that I would have been done toward the very beginning with the rejection of my family. I would have called it quits right then and there—threw my hands in the air and probably sobbed, something that is not normal for me! However, as I look deeper into this story of Joseph, a simple statement is made multiple times in Genesis 39 alone. It states in the first few verses of this chapter, *"**the Lord was with Joseph**, and he became a successful man, and he was in the house of his Egyptian master. His master saw **that the Lord was with him** and that the Lord caused all that he did to succeed in his hands. So Joseph found favor in his sight and attended him, and he made him overseer of his house and put him in charge of all that he had."*[13] I think it is normal to say that being rejected by your family hurts.

I think it is normal to say that it is not fair to have your family plot to kill you. I think that it is safe to say that no one is ready to be sold into slavery by their family. Yet with all that Joseph endured as a young man, he was able to begin his new life as a servant in Potiphar's house with a promise that we all need to be reminded of. "The Lord was with Joseph!"

> I have preached this for years as a life message, but while I was navigating through the most difficult season of my life, I found myself questioning many things related to my faith. Specifically, I began to question whether God was still with me?

The Lord was with Joseph as the most gripping events of his life were taking shape. The Lord was with Joseph when his brothers were making sarcastic and even hateful comments about him. The Lord was with Joseph as his brothers plotted to kill him. The Lord was with Joseph as he lay in a pit scared and alone. The Lord was with Joseph as the slave trader Ishmaelites took him captive. I have preached this for years as a life message, but while I was navigating through the most difficult season of my life, I found myself questioning many things related to my faith. Specifically, I began to question whether God was still with me?

Not long after we had departed the golf course via helicopter, I asked one of the paramedics about the hospital I was being transferred to. I was told that we would be heading to Valley Medical Hospital in Santa Clara, California. For some, that would be just a footnote. For me, I became immediately concerned due to my health insurance coverage. This hospital was "out of network," and I became more focused in my mind about the thousands of dollars I would be paying above and beyond my insurance deductibles. I would also later discover that since I had just finished college and had accepted a new position that allowed for health benefits, I would be caught in the middle of a transition season. This transition would eventually result in the immediate loss of coverage with both my former as well as my new insurance carriers. And while all of this was beginning to take shape without my knowledge, my personal stress was continuing to build without a true understanding of what would be ahead. But what I did not realize is that within the hour, this would be the least of my worries and none of it would be my focus any longer.

HOLE #5

Upon landing on the roof of Valley Medical Hospital, I was met by multiple emergency room personnel who began to shout over the sounds of the helicopter. I have witnessed these scenes in different television shows and movies, but I was now personally living it for the first time. It was organized chaos, and yet, everyone had a job to do and seemed to be doing it well. I was immediately taken from the rooftop entrance into an exam room and informed of the tests they were going to begin. I was asked to remain still during my first series of x-rays. Once they were complete, I was transferred to another area where I had my first series of CT scans. Following the CT scans, they began another series of tests that included my first set of MRI scans. During each set, the medical personnel asked me to "remain calm" and "don't move" so that they could capture the images for evaluation. Externally, I was doing my best to enjoy the moments with the hospital staff, but internally, I was still stressed about my finances—not my health. All I could process was the fact that each test they performed equaled thousands of dollars that I did not have. I was a former college student and rookie pastor with student loans that would be due in six months, and each x-ray, CT scan, MRI, and even the Band-Aids used would be added to an ever-growing bill.

At the conclusion of the first series of tests, I was transferred back to a small room surrounded by curtains. I don't remember how long I was alone, but it felt like an eternity. Eventually, a doctor came in and introduced himself to me. In addition to his name which I believe I mocked (something I do not recommend while others are holding your life in their hands physically or even metaphorically), this very kind and patient man announced that he was the on-call neurologist. If you had asked me then what a neurologist was or their function, I would have made something up. My meeting with him would be the first of the many miracle moments I would experience during this crisis. Had I been taken to the hospital that was within my insurance network, I would not have had access to this particular neurosurgeon. Today, I am grateful that my "out-of-network neurologist" who studied my nervous system and brain, was ranked in the top ten in the nation at that time. What began as a crisis in my head would prove to me that the same God that was with Joseph, was the same God who was walking with me!

> What began as a crisis in my head would prove to me that the same God that was with Joseph, was the same God who was walking with me!

As the neurologist began to speak, he began to hold up x-rays and charts from all the tests that had just been completed. In the middle of all his verbal summaries of these tests, it would be this doctor that would announce that I had "fractured my fourth vertebrae." I remember hearing the words but not understanding its meaning. Again, I knew that this would be a future sermon illustration, so I decided to take my liberties and enjoy the journey. I asked my doctor, "What does that mean?" He simply replied with, "Abe, you broke your neck." There were many thoughts that flooded my head. The first was, that can't be, I want a second opinion. But that was not what came out of my mouth. This may be an appropriate time to confess a weakness in my life. I have at times viewed it as a strength, but it has also resulted in me battling issues because of this struggle. My natural tendency then was to speak whatever entered my head as the first thought that would come out of my mouth. It has since improved, but not by much. A doctor had just stated that I had broken my neck and my inability to process this newly acquired information correctly caused me to yell, "…well, fix it!"

I don't think that my doctor was adequately prepared during his years of medical school for this type of response, especially coming from a guy who was lying flat on a medical gurney in front of him. When a doctor says you have "…broken your neck" and your reply is "…fix it," the conversation can go in many different directions. Thankfully, this doctor did not suffer from the same issues I did of blurting out his initial thoughts and comments within his head. He simply answered in surprise with one word, "What?" Both of us were a bit shocked and confused by each other's responses. In my attempt to be perfectly clear in my part of the communication, I said, "I didn't come here for a tour of the hospital doctor… FIX IT!" He smiled and settled in, knowing that I would be a patient who could test his patience and that this was going to be a process that required a greater sense of his attention. Reality was far from sinking in and he was very aware at that moment that we had a long road ahead. He patiently said, "Okay. There are multiple things that we are going to need to do. The first thing I need to talk to you about is a *halo*. Do you know what a *halo* is?" My first thought was, "I've grown up in church my entire life and now I'm a pastor. I've seen pictures of angels, I've seen movies depicting angels, I'm pretty sure I know what a halo is!" Again, reality was still far away. I was still in the mode of having fun with the entire hospital staff, so my quick response was, "Am I dying?"

My doctor quickly replied, "It's not that kind of halo! You see Abe, we need to drill four screws into your forehead. It will be attached to this horseshoe looking item that will surround your head. With the halo attached, we will secure it to a brace that will wrap around your chest. This device and procedure will help you because of the amount of swelling in your neck. It will lift the weight of your head off your neck allowing the swelling to subside over the next few weeks. After the swelling has gone down, we will be able to assess your surgery options."

Even though my doctor was so descriptive, and ever so thorough, there was only one thing that I heard. Out of all the words coming my way, my brain fixated on the doctor explaining that he was going to drill four screws into my head. Time stopped, my breathing sped up and I began to negotiate with him in a manner much different than I had previously communicated since arriving and being placed under his care. I pleaded with him to see what other options there were, including asking for a second opinion— anything but the screws. Unfortunately, there were no additional options available for me to consider.

This was my singular option and it felt as if time was of the essence. When I finally arrived at the point in which this was going to become reality, I asked if I "…would be placed under anesthesia?" It was my last hope of avoiding as much awareness of any screws being drilled into my head as possible. Then, as if I had not had enough trauma to my body and mind, my doctor looked at me and stated, "We don't have that kind of time. We will give you four local injections of Novocaine into your forehead." That was it. I had no choice. I decided right then to confess my faults. I told my doctor that I was scared of needles and did not like shots. Not at all. In fact, I was so afraid that I had always "lied about having a tetanus shot for the previous ten years so that I could avoid needles." I stated that my philosophy was to avoid stepping on rusty nails so that I would not ever need that shot. It was serious. Very serious! The words that came next helped me understand that I had the right doctor because of his humor. He said, "Son, by the time you are done with all that is coming, needles will be nothing."

As the medical team began to prepare the hardware that was going to be physically attached to my body, I still had no sense of true reality. To the best of my abilities, I was still joking with the staff and enjoying the setting, while internally, I was starting to become more and more nervous. Most would say that it would be natural, but my anxiety was only associated with my physical appearance. I was more concerned with how I would look with all of this hardware without realizing that the most life changing statement would not be revealed for another few hours.

As the procedure began, I can tell you that I yelled and screamed multiple times due to the *thought* of needles as opposed to the actual *pain* of the needles. I remember laying on the table as the doctor said, "It's time to begin." I remember saying "Do you use some kind of Black & Decker drill?" My doctor replied by saying, "…pretty much!" And with that, the drilling began. I can now admit that I didn't feel much due to the local anesthetic, but psychologically, I was struggling with the sound of a drill, feeling pressure on my skull, and then realizing the two sensations I was experiencing were actually related.

At the conclusion of the procedure, my doctor announced that they were complete and that it was time to transfer me to my room. As we began the journey down the long hall, I realized that my doctor was walking beside me. I don't know if this was or is a normal protocol or not, but I felt a bond and great comfort to have him close by based upon all that we had gone through together.

As I was being wheeled down the hall, we began to turn a corner upon which I noticed a mirror. Now, it's important to note that every hospital is equipped with large mirrors that are placed near the ceiling and at the intersection of each adjoining hall. The purpose of these mirrors is to prevent accidents within the hospital as patients are being transported from one point to another. The usage is not for a cosmetic purpose but rather a safety resource.

My eye caught one of these mirrors and at that very moment, I yelled "STOP!" My doctor quickly began to assess what was wrong physically while everyone else froze. I announced to everyone present, "I just saw a mirror and I want to move back a few feet to see what I look like." This amazing doctor, filled with great wisdom said, "Abe, I don't believe this is a good idea. You have experienced a significant amount of trauma and I don't believe it would be wise for you to look yet." I insisted and said, "I want to go back and see." The doctor paused, and then gave permission to the nurses transporting me to back up a few feet.

What I did not know or at least remember at that moment was that the mirror I was asking to look at was significantly different from the typical mirror found in a home, a store or even a restroom. The kinds of mirrors that are in hospital hallways are intended to give a 160-degree view of its surroundings. In order to accomplish this task, the images will look normal when you are further away. However, when you are up close, the image can and or will look distorted. Now, remember—at this point, I have significant hardware attached to my body and the first mirror that I am going to look at has the potential to distort my image. Ignoring the recommendation of my doctor, I looked. I shouldn't have, but I did and what I saw was awful! Part of my face looked as if it had been stretched (an illusion based on the angle of the mirror, I think). The screws were hard to see in full view but from my angle, I could notice that the points of contact for each screw had some liquid surrounding them. I would later learn that it was a gel used to prevent the screws from rusting, but I assumed it was the fluid from my brain beginning to drain. I was horrified! I was scared! I was mad! I looked at my doctor and said, "I can't believe that you would allow me to look at myself!" Without hesitation, he answered, "YOU ASKED!" I said, "Well, I don't want to see this, let's go… GO, GO, GO!" And with that, the medical team turned into my definition of a NASCAR pit car crew and with great speed took off immediately as far away from that evil mirror as possible. To this day, anytime that I see one of those mirrors, I do my best to avoid looking directly into it due to the extreme trauma of this one moment and a potential fear that I may see an image of myself that is probably my reality.

HOLE #6

When we arrived at the place that would become my hospital room, it was late into the evening and dark both outside and inside the room. I did not know at the time, but the room held four beds and there were two other patients already asleep for the night. I was asked to once again remain still as I was transferred from the mobile hospital gurney into my new hospital bed. However, this would not be a typical hospital bed. This bed had weights attached to it that the medical team began connecting to my newly installed hardware. The purpose was to anchor me in preventing any sudden movements that could cause further damage to my spinal cord. After the team finished my bed transfer, they left the room, allowing my doctor a private moment where he would remain a bit to make sure that I was settled.

He let me know that he was officially done with his shift but asked if I had any questions for him before he left for the evening? There were so many emotions, so many chapters that we had navigated in a matter of a few hours. But this intimate moment gave me a chance to let my guard down and be vulnerable with someone that I had just met. I said, "Doctor, I know that I have joked a lot and done my best to have some fun through this process. I guess my only question that I have for you is… when can I return back to my normal life?" I did not believe that to be a hard question or even one that would be considered odd. However, I remember looking at his face and noticing that even though the room was dark, there was enough light to notice that his reaction to my question had caused him concern. He answered with, "I don't believe I understand your question." I replied, "I want to know when I'll be able to return home, drive, go back to work, when can I return to my normal routine?" What he said next is where everything changed. This would have been another perfect moment for someone to yell "FORE!" because I had no clue of what was coming next.

My doctor's tone changed, and he stated, "Son, your definition of normal no longer exists. You see, since you've been in our hospital, you have not moved. Abe, you've been diagnosed as a quadriplegic and can't move anything from your neck down. You haven't probably noticed because everyone here during your exams, your x-rays, your scans, and the other procedures have all said the same thing, 'don't move!' The reality is, you have severe nerve damage and will likely never walk again." In that moment, I attempted to do something that formerly was very natural and second nature for me. I tried to move my hand attempting to wiggle my fingers. And to my surprise, nothing moved. I tried to wiggle my toes that I could see at the end of the bed, but they did not move. I tried to physically get out of bed forgetting that I was attached to a mechanism that anchored me down, but it did not matter. My brain had sent the message for movement to my body, but nothing responded. My doctor continued to speak during my private experiments without knowing that I was attempting to move. My intent was to be able to physically make some gesture to prove him wrong, but all it did was prove him to be right. I was paralyzed, unable to move. He continued, "I'm so sorry that you

> **As the physical light was switched to a night mode in the room, I felt as if the whole world surrounding me was growing darker and darker.**

didn't know. I thought they told you… I'm so sorry." And with that, he turned and began to walk out of the room. As he turned around, he touched a switch which caused the dim light to dim even more.

In one moment, everything had changed. As the physical light was switched to a night mode in the room, I felt as if the whole world surrounding me was growing darker and darker. I felt as if I was falling without any idea of when I was going to hit the bottom. Hours earlier, I had felt invincible with my entire life in front of me. And now, I was lying in a hospital room wondering if this was going to be my new norm? Every dream I had ever dreamt felt as if they were being flushed away with each second that was passing. The pastoral call of God on my life to be a minister felt as if it was now gone. There was no way a church could keep a quadriplegic pastor. There would be nothing that I was currently doing as a Youth and Music Pastor that I could physically be able to continue. And as that dream was vanishing, the one that hit me hardest was marriage. I had a beautiful girlfriend who I knew God had brought to my life. There was no way that I could ever consider asking her to marry me, knowing that it would be a life-sentence to become my caregiver on day one. The conversations we had about our future together felt as if they were fading as well. The dream of children with her was

> The thought of forever was gone because the only thing in front of me was a diagnosis.

fading. The thought of forever was gone because the only thing in front of me was a diagnosis.

I don't believe that I understood then what I do now about the words diagnosis and prognosis. My assumption was that they were the same or at least similar in meaning. I quickly learned that there was a difference. The definition of the word diagnosis is: "A determining or analysis of the cause or nature of a problem or situation."[14] A diagnosis is the result of some phenomenon. The definition of the word prognosis is: "A forecasting of the probable course and outcome of a disease, especially of the chances of recovery."[15] One identifies the problem while the other is a prediction of what will develop. I assumed that my issue was the diagnosis of a broken neck. I wasn't prepared for the prognosis of a life-change as a quadriplegic.

> In our moments of despair, hope is restored when we realize that He is with us.

I believe that there are moments throughout our lives where we can feel as if the circumstances in front of us are unfair. It is common to look at ourselves and wonder why I have to go through this when others are able to live "normal" lives? The crisis will always enter when we move from a place of unfairness to a state of despair. It's the moment where we accept that the prognosis is far greater than the diagnosis and we begin to slip into a deeper pit.

36

Returning back to the life of Joseph in scripture, the pain he had endured based upon the verbal abuse of family, a plot to kill him, a life change as he was sold into slavery and taken into a foreign land, and much more, should have depressed him. When we arrive at the end of this very chapter, it reads, *"But the Lord was with Joseph and showed him steadfast love and gave him favor in the sight of the keeper of the prison. And the keeper of the prison put Joseph in charge of all the prisoners who were in the prison. Whatever was done there, he was the one who did it. The keeper of the prison paid no attention to anything that was in Joseph's charge, because the Lord was with him. And whatever he did, the Lord made it succeed."* [16]

Despair means we have lost hope! As hope was quickly fading in my life based upon my personal crisis, there was an anchor I was trying to find. It would take weeks before I would discover this hope associated with Genesis

> Sadly, in my initial moments of a diagnosis and prognosis, all I heard was what a medical professional stated. Those words overshadowed the hope and promise that is rooted in God's Word.

39. In our moments of despair, hope is restored when we realize that He is with us. I have declared this message for years since my accident. The same God that was with Joseph is the same God that was with me during my moment of despair. The same God that was with Joseph in the middle of issues with his family; the

same God that was with Joseph as his brothers plotted murder; the same God that was with Joseph as he was sold into slavery; the same God that was with Joseph as he landed in Potiphar's house; the same God that was with Joseph in the moments of temptation; the same God that was with Joseph as he was falsely accused; the same God that was with Joseph as he was sent to prison with a life-sentence; the same God that was with Joseph as he was forgotten by others... the same God that was with Joseph is the same God that was and still is with me... He is the same God that is with you in this place of despair!

> Oftentimes, tragedy makes us believe that our lives would be significantly better if we could go back in time and change the last bad event in our lives.

The natural reaction would be to assume that a diagnosis/prognosis is actually a new life sentence. If a doctor speaks it based upon their expertise, their extensive scientific research and background, then it is to become a reality. Sadly, in my initial moments of a diagnosis and prognosis, all I heard was what a medical professional stated. Those words overshadowed the hope and promise that is rooted in God's Word. Those words eclipsed what I knew to be my reality and the foundation of faith that had sustained my life till that point and still reaches out to this very day.

Oftentimes, tragedy makes us believe that our lives would be significantly better if we could go back in time and change the last bad event in our lives. In my life, many would assume that my changeup would be to not get into that very golf cart at that particular moment. While that makes sense practically, physically, and even financially, I am able to see what God did in the many moments, days, weeks, months, and years to follow that stem from that one accident. If I could not avoid the accident that changed my life, I believe that the next greatest change I would have made would be what I would choose to focus upon in the middle of my crisis.

> God's Word is what we are to hide and store in the same way we would a valuable treasure. It must be guarded in a place that no one else has access to.

HOLE #7

The words of a doctor were all I could hear, that quickly caused every other word to disappear. I don't believe that I realized how easy it is to allow the words of others to overshadow the promises of God's Word. These are the very words that I have read, memorized, and stored in my heart to guide me through these moments of crisis. Again, I reflect back on the life of Joseph from Genesis 39. Little did he know that each moment of great crisis would lead him to experience the favor of God. One thing that separates us today from Joseph, is the privilege of being refocused in the middle of crisis through the lens of God's Word. Joseph never had the chance to read what we have access to in scripture. What we have available to us today in God's Word, has far greater value than any earthly possession we could acquire.

Scripture says, *"I have stored up your word in my heart, that I might not sin against you."*[17] The Hebrew word used to describe the phrase "stored up" or hide is "צָפַן or tsaphan"[18] (Don't check out because I just quoted a biblical language!) I share this word with you because it is stronger than our English definition of the word "hide." For us, "hide" is something you do while playing a game or avoiding contact with someone you don't want to see (hypothetically—something I may or may not have done). God's Word is what we are to hide and store in the same way we would a valuable treasure. It must be guarded in a place that no one else has access to. It will be God's Word that will then emerge when we need it the most. In our moments of crisis, His Word will be our strength. In our moments of temptations, His Word will be our strength. In our moments of struggle, His Word will be our strength and will cause our focus to

> If you are in a state of shock based upon the crisis words of another, I challenge you to lift your eyes beyond your situation and look to God's Word.

become clearer. There would be no guarantee of what was ahead for me beyond a diagnosis. But a hope would eventually surface based upon God's Word that was stored in my heart for the many unknown moments ahead. If you are in a state of shock based upon the crisis words of another, I challenge you to lift your eyes beyond your situation and look to God's Word. His Word will guide you when you feel lost. His Word will refresh you when you feel dry. His Word will comfort you when you have suffered loss. His Word will be the singular thing to restore a sense of focus when all you see is despair.

STAGE 3

Prepare

"Golf can best be defined as an endless series of tragedies obscured by the occasional miracle."[19]
—Unknown Author

I have experienced the reality of what happens when a series of events causes you to move from the general feeling of life being unfair to an actual mental state of despair. An accumulation of disappointment, fear, discouragement, and even anger can ever so easily evolve into a dark and dangerous place. I have heard many leaders over the years say that "we choose daily to be *bitter* or *better*." While this is a powerful truth and a great life habit, there must be a moment where we

> There must be a moment where we intentionally choose to not just be better, but we choose to be strong through the power of Christ.

intentionally choose to not just be better, but we choose to be strong through the power of Christ. I believe that there is a difference between being brave and being strong. Bravery happens in the midst of crisis or fear. It's the moment when we should be filled with fear, but we somehow, some way, pull it together to be "brave." Being strong requires preparation—whether it is physically, like lifting weights at the gym or emotionally choosing to be "better," you can only be as strong as you are prepared for. When life progresses past the place of unfairness into the place of despair, it is vital that we are prepared. For me, the best time to begin to prepare for what is ahead is before it's too late.

> Crisis does not give us the chance to adequately prepare because most crises arrive unexpectedly. The personal preparation for the times of tribulation, crisis, and unexpected tragedies must occur in our private time with Jesus.

With all of this, preparation is the key for this to become our reality. We know this principle and use it every day. For example, when I am leaving on a trip, I do not have the luxury of packing after I have departed. I am required to plan or prepare prior to a trip so that I leave ready. Many times, it is in the last moments as procrastination is my norm, but that is beside the point. Crisis does not give us the chance to adequately prepare because most crises arrive unexpectedly. The personal preparation for the times of tribulation, crisis, and unexpected tragedies must occur in our private time with Jesus.

There is a passage of scripture that has become special to me as I look back on this season of my life. Psalm 40:2 says, *"He drew me up from the pit of destruction, out of the miry bog, and set my feet upon a rock, making my steps secure."*[20] King David had been reflecting on how long he had to wait before God delivered him from his enemies and from King Saul. Unlike Joseph who we looked at earlier, David had never been in a physical pit. The pit he was referring to was a picture of the difficult years that he had endured. "The pit" is also a term for *Sheol*, the realm of the dead. David's life was in a constant state of danger and the potential of death at the hand of King Saul was most likely imminent. And yet, I do not believe that the preparation for David's battles happened on the spot—the preparation began long before his journey had begun. It happened while standing in a shepherd's field caring for sheep. His preparation was fighting the wild animals that threatened him and the livestock under his care. It happened in his quiet time of worship and prayer. It happened while he was in a waiting period that was not wasted but became his training ground for his unknown journey to the throne, and the decades beyond.

I would love to tell you that I was well prepared for anything life could throw at me upon entering my physical crisis while lying in a hospital room. I wish that I could say that I really was as invincible as I had previously felt, but there is nothing further from the truth. As I was lying in a room that was continually growing darker every second, I had no clue of what was happening in a waiting room just down the hall.

A large group of friends and church family members had arrived and were waiting for some news about my condition. These friends were praying and spiritually preparing themselves—and even me—for the journey ahead even though they knew nothing of the diagnosis because they were not related to me as family members.

Thinking about it today, I wonder if that moment of chaos in my life would have been different if one of them were standing in the room? None of them were given immediate access or allowed a chance to communicate with me at that point, so, the feeling of isolation, crisis, and great confusion was mine alone to process. This was a new feeling to me, and I was completely overwhelmed. During the moments after my doctor had left the room, I began to cry out to God. The phrase, "cry out to God" is a church phrase that Christians use to indicate intentional imploring of and communication to God for His presence and His will. I do not believe that definition would describe my cries at that particular time to God. My cries were ones of complaints and defense of my life prior to that point.

I began to argue with God, convincing Him of my faithfulness to Him. I began to speak of my journey as a boy who volunteered to run the overhead projector (if you know, you know) at the age of eight for my church. I began to plead with Him about His pastoral call that He had revealed to me, which I could no longer fulfill because of my prognosis. I began to argue about my faithfulness to serve Him as a teenager who played the piano for our church and now was a staff pastor in that same church. It is embarrassing to admit it today, but sadly, I was quoting my resume to the Creator of the Universe in my moments of desperation.

HOLE #8

I believe that desperation causes us to cling to things that were previously familiar. Reciting my accomplishments to my Heavenly Father in that moment was the equivalent of yelling at a referee at a sporting event for a bad call that we did not agree with. This is something I have done and continue to do in the middle of every sporting event connected to my three sons. Not the greatest testimony of a pastor, but I do feel satisfied knowing that the world has heard my objection. Yelling may make us feel better, but I have never observed or even personally experienced a referee changing their call just because of the loudest voice of opposition. Pleading my case to God was not a prayer request, it was an accusation of my unfair treatment. Something like this was not supposed to happen to someone like me. Typing it today is the revelation of pride, arrogance, ignorance, and much more. I was in my "pit moment," and all I could see, or process, was the injustice of the moment. Thankfully, there would be a personal breaking

> I believe that desperation causes us to cling to things that were previously familiar.

moment in the multiple days ahead that prevented me from remaining in this unhealthy state.

For the next several hours, well past midnight, I was in and out of sleep. Each time I would wake, I was greeted by another friendly face and still had the presence of friends and Anna. A few hours later, my parents and sister arrived after driving nine hours straight from another state. Each time another group would arrive, someone would have to begin the story again by sharing the details that few people fully understood—including myself.

When I woke up later the next morning to begin my first full day in the hospital, I realized that the room I was in was not a private room. With all of the activity, I had not noticed a man directly across from me, another man in a bed in my right corner and an empty bed to my immediate right. The one thing that we three men had in common was that all of us were suffering from an accident that resulted in a broken neck. The difference was how we broke it. The person across from me had broken his neck in a motorcycle accident. He had taken a tight corner at high speeds ejecting him from his bike and sending him through two fences before he finally stopped. The other young man was there due to a mountain-climbing accident. All three of us had screws drilled into our heads and halos attached, but I was the only one whose accident was not as noteworthy as theirs was. Their accidents by comparison seemed adventurous, daring, and understandable. My accident involved a golf cart, something that is seen as low impact and truly embarrassing by contrast.

HOLE #9

In one of the many quiet instances in which I began to calm my heart and mind down, I began to notice music playing softly in the background. This was not the normal elevator or lounge music that we expect to hear in lobbies or even in hospitals. This music was familiar. This music was different. This was worship! Powerful, calming, healing, worship. Many have limited the definition of worship to church attendance, participation in a faith-related activity, or a segment of songs sung during a church service. To summarize worship into these types of practices is to truly limit the scope and power found in godly worship. Not only have I experienced the true impact of authentic worship, but I was also blessed to be surrounded in these moments by family and friends who knew that true worship would change everything I was facing despite their knowledge of my new revelation.

Worship culture has the power to shift the atmosphere of everything we are navigating. It is amazing what happens when we are willing and able to lift our eyes off our present-day circumstances and focus them on both the greatness and goodness of God. At this season of my ministry career, the word worship was a part of the official employment title I carried, but it would be this crisis that would teach me about the power of worship. The worship music playing was on a continual repeat cycle, so I still have no idea of how long it had been playing prior to me noticing. What I did know was that it was familiar.

The CD that was on repeat was a personal favorite at that time. The worship album was titled "Shout to the Lord" and had reached best-selling worship album status in that season. In an article I would read years later, the composer and lead vocalist stated that the title track was written during a period in which she was at rock bottom. She stated, "I wrote it when I was feeling discouraged. I felt I could either scream and pull my hair out, or praise God."[21] I wish that I had known the genesis of this song during my dark moments. In addition to the title track was another song titled, "Jesus, Lover of My Soul." This song had become my all-time favorite as a worship leader at that time. This was not just a song I had enjoyed. This was a song that I had led and played hundreds of times for several years as a worship leader. This very song happened to be playing at the moment I noticed and recognized music in my hospital room. As the song was playing, I became aware—almost for the first time—the depth of the lyrics that I had sung for so long. The portion of the song that captured my

> It is amazing what happens when we are willing and able to lift our eyes off our present-day circumstances and focus them on both the greatness and goodness of God.

heart was the quoting of Psalm 40:2. "You've taken me from the miry clay, set my feet upon a rock..." The chorus continued: "I love you, I need you, though my world may fall, I'll never let you go..."

These words sound poetic and nice but contain an element of both the promises of God and faith declarations that I needed. I had sung and even led that song hundreds of times, but up until that moment, I had never been forced to live those words out. I had never been in miry clay. At that moment, I don't think I comprehended what miry clay was? My world had never fallen, and I had never been tempted to let go of God. But in one moment, everything had changed. My world was falling and felt as if it was not stopping. My feet were stuck in miry clay, and it felt as if I was sinking, which is even worse when you are paralyzed and can't move your feet to escape. In a moment of true desperation, I surrendered.

When Christians hear the word "surrender" in relation to the things of Christ, we assume it is healthy. Surrender is what we as Christians do to place Christ at the center of our lives. It then is no longer my agenda, but His agenda. It is not my will, but His will working to be accomplished in and through my life. Surrender sounds noble for the Christ-follower, but my surrender was the opposite. My surrender was not healthy. My surrender was the equivalent to a general on a battlefield who had two options, death or surrender. My surrender became a prayer of defeat as opposed to a prayer of faith.

I literally prayed, "God, if this is your plan for my life...then I guess I will be a quadriplegic who worships you!" In reflecting upon that kind of prayer today, I know it was not a faith-filled prayer. Again, it could be interpreted as noble, but it was a prayer of loss and concession. It is a prayer that I celebrate as one rooted in worship, but also one that represents a moment that I was giving up. Regardless of the quality of that prayer, I closed my eyes and went to sleep. My sleep was not associated with a theme of peace. It was fatigue and drugs. It was a sleep that was so deep that when I woke up a few moments (maybe hours) later, I startled myself.

HOLE #10

My sadness upon waking was realizing that this was not a dream. When you wake from a sudden sleep and try to process where you are at, I believe it becomes natural to perform minor tests. In that moment, I discovered that I still could not move from the neck down. There were still four screws sticking out of my head attached to a body brace. I was still lying in a hospital room, but I did notice that something had changed. Where I at one point had been left alone in my room, I now realized that I was no longer alone. I now noticed a few nurses surrounding my bed.

It's important to note that I remain grateful for the amazing medical personnel that worked with me during those initial moments of tragedy, as well as the years of follow-up appointments and care. However, the moment that would immediately follow my awakening from this sleep and interaction with a nurse, would not be my finest exchange of words. Something I have also realized since, is that my revelation of nothing changing upon waking is what quickly set me back into my downward faithless struggle. When the two nurses that were surrounding my bed had realized that I was awake, they began to communicate with me to offer me care. I don't remember much of the initial conversation, but I do remember their kindness and the willingness of one of them to offer me "ice chips." Let me stop for a second and say this—if you do not know what ice chips are, then I believe you are truly missing out. They are a hospital staple and due to the injury that I had suffered, I was not allowed any solid food to eat. The only thing I could have— ice chips—thin pieces of ice that I could place in my mouth without causing fear for the medical team of my choking. When I finally acknowledged my desire for another helping of previously explained ice chips (my one joy in the midst of my very real crisis), one of the nurses left the room to bring more back.

If you would have told me that a miracle moment was ahead, I would never have believed it. Doctors would later say that while the potential of any feeling, sensation, or mobility to my limbs could be a possibility, it was highly unlikely. Again, my concept of hope had diminished and was growing thinner with each passing minute. In my life, I have realized that the miracle moments that I have experienced have arrived in the center of God's perfect timing. Though God's timing is always perfect, it always comes as a shock and surprise in my life. The kind of miracle I needed would be one that many have prayed for, and yet, never experienced. Because it was more common to hear of the news of individuals who were tragically impacted by major accidents, I had no thoughts or hope of my condition changing or shifting. But little did I know, there was a miracle moment that was seconds away from beginning that would not only change the prognosis of my life, but it would also shock my family, my friends, and the entire medical community working on my case. It would also be the first moment since landing on the rooftop of this hospital where a sense of hope would begin to shine through. Who would have thought that ice chips would become a part of a miracle?

> In my life, I have realized that the miracle moments that I have experienced have arrived in the center of God's perfect timing. Though God's timing is always perfect, it always comes as a shock and surprise in my life.

HOLE #11

As I was lying on my back, unable to move, I happened to notice the pitcher that contained the original ice chips I had previously been offered. I could not move because of my paralysis, but I was aware that they were close. As I looked at the pitcher that was to my left, and the nurse that was on my right, I decided that I no longer wanted to wait. I decided that I needed them now. Despite my inner urgency, I kindly said, "Excuse me? I was hoping to have some of the ice chips over there" (trying to motion with my head, but to no avail due to it being anchored down—screws and all). The remaining nurse absently replied without any eye contact, "The nurse went to grab some and will be back soon." I knew this, but there was no need to wait for someone else because there was a full pitcher right there! But how do you communicate in a dark room while you are paralyzed and unable to move? So, I restated "…the ice chips are over there" (again trying to motion without moving). What happened next caused me—a slightly frustrated patient—to begin to boil into a fully exasperated patient. The nurse said "Where?" and I was truly blown away. This lady who had the freedom of movement in all four of her limbs was asking a patient who was anchored to a bed where a pitcher of ice was! I then said, "It's right there to my left." With that directive, the nurse turned in the opposite direction to my right which was her left. Out of increasing frustration I said, "Your other left!"

Let me say, one thing that I did not understand at that point was the power a nurse has over a patient. This was my first hospital stay as an adult, and what should have been basic knowledge was not easy for me to process fast. This very kind nurse began to voice her frustration with me by saying, "…if you can just wait a few moments, I'm sure the nurse will return with your ice chips." In that moment, my peak of frustration reached a new height and I snapped. I realized that this would be my new definition of normal for the rest of my life as a quadriplegic and it was too much. For the remainder of my life, I would be at the mercy of anyone within proximity of my body, a body that could no longer function. My inability to move would subject me to the personalities and discernment of those sent to assist me. And worse, I would be limited in my ability as a communicator to clearly articulate my needs. While this should be simple for a pastor, I was obviously not doing well in my first moments as a quadriplegic.

Out of anger, I yelled back at my nurse (not recommended, but these were extenuating circumstances), "IT'S RIGHT THERE." In response the nurse yelled back (not professional, but understood), "WHERE?" And for a few moments, we exchanged the same words back and forth as both of our voices were escalating in sound. With one final plea, I yelled, "IT'S RIGHT THERE!" But this time something changed. A pulse shot through my body, filled my arm that caused it to raise and motion toward the left with my pointer finger fully extended at the existing pitcher of ice chips. In that moment, both the nurse and I froze. Something had changed and both of us were trying to process what had just happened. She froze because quadriplegic patients are not supposed to move anything from the neck down. I froze for a different reason. I was scared that for the remainder of my life, I would be frozen in this very posture with my arm extended and my finger pointing toward the left. Time stopped and then started back in slow motion. I had no idea of what had changed, but it was the first time in which the dark world that I had been living in had a small crack of light beginning to appear.

After a few seconds, the shock wore off a bit and I decided that I needed to see if I was able to move again. I quickly formulated a plan—I would count to three and see if I could wiggle the finger that had just pointed. I was scared and truly overwhelmed while trying to process what this could possibly mean. Was there a possibility that I would not be a quadriplegic? Was this supposed to happen? I had to know. In my head, I began to count 1... 2... 3 and in that very moment, my finger moved. My brain sent the message for my arm to move and—it did! My right arm and fingers began to move. I began to feel my feet and toes. Within a few moments, everything except for my left arm had regained all feeling and range of motion.

While this was all going on, I failed to notice that the nurse who engaged with me in a yelling match had quickly exited my room to find the on-call doctor for that particular shift. Not long after, she and a doctor rushed back into my room. The doctor began to examine me and verified that feeling had returned to my body. Though everything was weak from the impact of major trauma, I had all feeling returned back with the exception of my left arm. I was amazed and overwhelmed but still managed to go back to sleep due to the amount of trauma and drugs administered. When I woke up a few moments later, there was a steady flow of people in my room, joining Anna who refused to leave my side.

Though my room had a steady flow of traffic of family and friends, none of them would understand the extreme emotions that I was processing. They had no understanding of the total despair that I had experienced. All they knew was that I had fractured my fourth vertebrae and that surgery would be coming. The urgency and panic remained, but it seemed as if the major crisis had faded even though one arm was still unresponsive.

As the days continued, my original neurosurgeon who had given me exceptional care as I landed the previous night, decided to check in with me. He reexamined my charts, reread his notes, and began to catalog the miraculous improvements I had experienced in less than twenty-four hours. He then made a statement that has remained with me to this day. He said, "Abe, there is no scientific explanation as to why you have movement in your body. However, after nearly forty years of medical experience, I can tell you that I have seen signs that prove that there is a Being that is higher than us." I smiled and said, "Doctor, His name is Jesus, and He is my Healer!" He smiled back and responded, "Well maybe it's because you are a pastor." I quickly replied, "I have feeling in my body despite the fact that I am a pastor!"

My doctor informed me that we were going to begin some therapy over the next several weeks waiting for surgery. He said that once I completed surgery, I would be restarting the therapy processes from scratch. Over the next several days, I was unhooked from my bed anchors and given a wheelchair. My job was to begin to wheel myself around learning to maneuver accordingly. Even though I would not be restricted to a wheelchair, it was safer for me to use it while I was learning to balance all the additional hardware attached to me. Over the next several days, I spent time in physical and occupational therapy. While I was making great progress, I did not understand the psychological impact of trauma on my life. It would not be until a social worker arrived later to begin working with me.

After this social worker had introduced herself, she began to ask many questions related to my condition. Some of the questions included, "How are you feeling today? How are you adjusting to a wheelchair? How are you processing everything?" All of my answers were simple but firm statements, no more than one-word answers. Everything was progressing until she switched the focus from how I was feeling to my long-term plans. The questions changed a bit and she started asking me about my living space, "Where do you live? Does your apartment have stairs? Do you live alone?" I was slightly confused. I thought I was supposed to walk again. I began to wonder why all these questions did not apply to the miracle I had received that changed my condition? After a while, it became apparent that because I had experienced a miraculous recovery in such a short period, no one had updated my medical records. My charts still held my diagnosis as a quadriplegic.

The social worker's final question before I realized my charts had not changed was, "Abe, what plans do you need to begin to consider for your life change?" I quickly responded, "What do you mean?" She said, "With your diagnosis as a quadriplegic, there is no way you will be able to return to an upstairs apartment." Without thinking, I reached down, unbuckled my wheelchair seatbelt, and slowly stood to my feet. I looked down at the social worker whose face had dramatically changed expressions and I announced, "Do I look like a quadriplegic?" I was proving a valid point, but please keep in mind that I was wearing a hospital gown and had a halo screwed into my head attached to a body brace. Nevertheless, I was standing, and quadriplegic patients are not able to do that. The social worker quickly stood to her feet with eyes wide and said, "I will be right back."

What should have been a moment of triumph, instead, caused me to feel a greater sense of loss. As I carefully sat back down in my wheelchair, I began to tear up. I only had one hand that was able to move so I could not hide my tears very well. I wheeled myself out of the gym, down the hall and back to my room.

As I began to climb into bed, I found myself crying uncontrollably. There was nothing wrong. I was making progress. However, all I could see and process was what was in front of me.

HOLE #12

In a season of crisis, most of us can only see the issues we are facing. A sincere heart to grow after this crisis began to produce something new within me related to the theme of preparation. Today, I pray for the very best and prepare for the very worst for any situation I am walking into. That may sound very pessimistic, but it has become the balance between my faith posture and a posture of action. Both the best and the worst situations require the believer to engage in prayer. Without prayer, it is impossible to navigate our battles.

> Both the best and the worst situations require the believer to engage in prayer. Without prayer, it is impossible to navigate our battles.

Years ago, I read an article on the theme of prayer. It began by quoting an African proverb. *"Every morning a gazelle gets up knowing it must outrun the fastest lion or it will be eaten. And every morning a lion gets up knowing it must outrun the slowest gazelle or it will starve to death. So, whether you are a gazelle or a lion, every morning when you get up, you'd better be running."*[22] Beginning everyday with the discipline and need for prayer is what sustains me and helps me begin "running" into the day ahead. But normally, it is in the middle of crisis that I feel that it is easier to find and even make the time to pray. Hebrews 4:14-16 says, *"Since then we have a great high priest who has passed through the heavens, Jesus, the Son of God, let us hold fast our confession. For we do not have a high priest who is unable to sympathize with our weaknesses, but one who in every respect has been tempted as we are, yet without sin. Let us then with confidence draw near to the throne of grace, that we may receive mercy and find grace to help in time of need."*[23]

> As a follower of Christ, prayer must be my posture of preparation! To have the adequate preparation needed to navigate our battles will require us to pray prior to our crisis, not just after.

As a follower of Christ, prayer must be my posture of preparation! To have the adequate preparation needed to navigate our battles will require us to pray prior to our crisis, not just after. Most find and make time to pray in the middle of issues. Engaging in the power of daily prayer regardless of the things that we are facing prepares us for the unexpected.

Warfare

"Golf is a game in which you yell 'FORE,"
shoot six and write down five."
—Paul Harvey [24]

For many years following my accident, I assumed that the worst moment was the accident itself. What took me years to realize was that my golf accident would become the tip of the iceberg. There would be a series of events that would propel me into a deeper and even darker hole that I did not have any control of. I had so much to be thankful for. My ability to move my entire body except for my left arm was truly miraculous. The future was incredibly bright, but all I could see was my present circumstances. It's again my reminder that looking down will only focus on what's present but looking up to our Heavenly Father will restore hope when it has all faded.

> It's again my reminder that looking down will only focus on what's present but looking up to our Heavenly Father will restore hope when it has all faded.

With everything that I had encountered, I finally arrived at the point of surgery. About two weeks had passed since the date of my accident allowing the swelling in my neck to subside. Two weeks of physical and occupational therapy in a hospital. Two weeks of a few high moments surrounding my life with the remainder of them as low moments that no one knew I was privately battling. Two weeks that felt as if I was making progress only to have surgery reset the entire clock.

When I began the conversation with my neurosurgeon about this surgery, he began to share the risks at hand and his personal professional intentions. Any spinal cord surgery contains great risks, but this surgeon who had been with me from the beginning committed to work with me to prevent me limited long-term issues if possible. This surgery was a spinal fusion. The spinal fusion required my neurosurgeon to take a graph of my hip bone and insert it in my neck. He stated that they would be taking the equivalent of titanium thread and would be fusing my third, fourth and fifth vertebrae together using a piece of my hip to stabilize the fracture. Still to this day, I am in awe of what doctors say and how I interpret what they say. This doctor said he would fuse my vertebrae together using my hip and I began to mentally sing my new version of an old song, "The hip bone connected to the... neck bone?" (It's normal if you just sang it in your head!)

As we began to discuss the risks, he began to talk more about my profession as a pastor. At that time, I was a youth and music pastor. This meant I not only needed my voice to speak, but I also needed my voice to sing. My doctor said, "...we are going to attempt to do this surgery from the backside [of the neck] to protect your vocal cords. If we are not having success with the access we need from behind, we will have to go through the front. Based on your profession, I want to do everything that I can to protect your vocal cords, but I want you to know all of the possibilities that we may encounter." I quickly responded, "I don't like my singing voice much... are you able to help me with that while you're in there?" My response made him smile but in reality, was my attempt to cover another fear of the unknown coming my way.

As surgery was about to begin, I was given one additional possibility. I was told that if they needed to go through the front, I may wake up with a tube in my mouth. They said, "...many people don't like the feeling of this and some, without realizing it, attempt to pull it out. If you wake up with a tube in your mouth, don't be alarmed." I had four screws sticking out of my head, the possibilities of large incisions on the front and back of my neck, the possibility of paralysis returning to my body due to the surgery; they were now taking a piece of my hip out and finally, they did not want me to be alarmed about the possibility of a tube in my mouth. It made perfect sense to not be alarmed!

With that as the final instruction, I was assigned the task that many have experienced prior to surgical procedures... counting backwards. I was asked to count backwards from ten down to one to test the anesthesia that had already been administered to my body. I have always wondered if there is any purpose to that or if there are bets in the room to see how far down the patient will count. I don't believe I made it past eight, but I'm truly thankful that it worked.

HOLE #13

Surgery lasted between four to five hours. During this time, family and friends were waiting and agreeing in prayer for a miracle moment again. When I was awakened from surgery while in the recovery room, I did what I assumed most normal people would do based on the details of the last thing they heard prior to going to sleep. I began to lick my lips and began using my tongue to try to see if there was a tube coming out of my mouth (it's ok if you just began to do this!). To repeat this motion over and over in front of medical personnel will cause them to look at you with concern. Finally, my neurosurgeon walked up to me. He noticed my repeated mouth actions, processed what I was attempting to figure out on my own and finally said, "Abe, there is no tube in your mouth. Surgery was very successful! We were able to go through the back of your neck and did not even come close to your vocal cords. Everything is fine!" It provided some relief which caused me to close my eyes and go back to sleep.

Recovery from any surgery is difficult under normal circumstances. I not only had the task of recovery from a spinal fusion, but I was also now missing a portion of my hip due to the surgery. This would later translate into the task of learning to walk again, something I had no idea I would be facing. While both of these are traumatic, nothing prepared me for the bed that I was transferred to post surgery. While waking up in the intensive care unit, still laying on my back and unaware of my surroundings, my neurosurgeon informed me that a typical post operation concern are blood clots. According to the Mayo Clinic, "Blood clots form when platelets (blood components) and plasma proteins thicken, forming a semisolid mass.[25]" I don't understand what any of that means, but I was told that inactivity may cause a blood clot to form. In order to prevent and account for this, I had already been transferred to a rotating bed.

If you have never heard or understand the concept of a rotating bed, then you understand the shock and confusion that I had experienced in that moment. The bed that I was strapped to, had the ability to turn on its longitudinal axes (or rotate side to side.) I was told that they were going to activate the bed beginning with a 90-degree radius. As the bed began to move, I began to yell. I no longer felt the pain from surgery, I was now moving towards the floor while still having a halo attached to my head. I would have no ability to brace myself when I would most definitely fall out of this bed. After my first 180-degree rotation from my right to my left side, I was able to cause so much commotion that the medical staff stopped the bed. There was much trauma that I apparently was inflicting upon this staff, that they began to work on another solution. Little did they know that I would assert myself into their discussion and leverage all negotiating skills on my behalf. Upon "debating" the need for this device, we settled on a 45-degree angle maximum. My argument was that I had already broken my neck, how bad could a blood clot really be?

As the bed began to rotate, I began to settle in with my new surroundings and my new norm. My assumption was that we would only use this bed for a few minutes every hour and then I would be able to go back to the joy of laying still. No one had the courage to admit that it would not be a few minutes every hour, but that I would be rotating consistently for the next forty-eight hours without a pause. I would be lying if I said that I handled this portion of recovery with great strength and perseverance. Instead, I yelled for the majority of the two days having to be reminded many times that I was a pastor due to my choice of words sporadically used. Although this is not a conversation that my family brings up today, I still blame it on the pain medication that I was on which dulled all senses and rationale. Thankfully, what felt like a hopeless situation eventually concluded and my bout with a rotating bed was done.

HOLE #14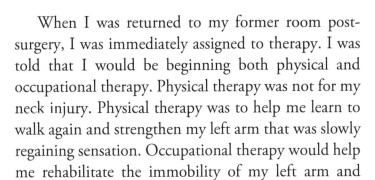

When I was returned to my former room post-surgery, I was immediately assigned to therapy. I was told that I would be beginning both physical and occupational therapy. Physical therapy was not for my neck injury. Physical therapy was to help me learn to walk again and strengthen my left arm that was slowly regaining sensation. Occupational therapy would help me rehabilitate the immobility of my left arm and hand with greater function.

To be assigned to physical therapy for walking made no sense to me whatsoever. I had no problem walking before my accident and now it was an apparent issue. I didn't understand how much of an issue it was until I was stood up by two medical staff members and a hoist. They moved me in between two parallel bars so that I would be able to have additional support. Again, I was not prepared for what came next. My therapist said, "We are going to have you take a step." My response was, "No problem!" hoping that I would be able to prove that I did not need this. As I took my first step, a significant pain shot from my hip into my lower back and then rapidly spread throughout my entire body. I yelled (as I had done multiple times throughout this process) which caused both staff members to immediately support me lifting the weight of my body off my feet. I was then navigated back to my wheelchair for a moment of rest. Instead of continuing with this therapy, which was recommended, I requested to end my first day of physical therapy after a few moments and one failed attempt to walk. Due to their concern of fatigue based on my comments, I was wheeled back to my room.

Fatigue, however, was not the true issue that I was dealing with as I was returned to my room. It was hopelessness! When God's people have an inability to see the hope that is always present, we begin to battle on another level. Prior to my accident, I heard a pastor share a story about the loss of hope connected to world history. It was the Battle of Waterloo that would mark the end of Napoleon's military career due to his defeat by the Duke of Wellington. "On June 18, 1815, Napoleon led his army of 72,000 troops against the 68,000-man British army."[26] For many throughout England, Wellington was their last hope for victory. The charisma of Napoleon and his return to power caused many European nations to have great concern.

> When God's people have an inability to see the hope that is always present, we begin to battle on another level.

In our present-day culture, we enjoy the luxury or burden of instant breaking news through the advancement of technology in our homes, our cars, on our phones, and even our watches. That is obviously not a luxury that was available in the 1800s. The only options they had to send out a mass message would require the use of a sailing ship at sea. That ship would send whatever message they wanted to communicate through the usage of signals with coded flags or lights. The message or breaking news would be relayed to a signalman on top of a Cathedral, typically one of the highest points in a town or city. It is said that on the evening of June 18, 1815, the status of the Battle of Waterloo began to be relayed to a signalman on top of the Winchester Cathedral. As the message came in, they began to spell out a message determining England's future. As the letters were being assembled and then displayed, the crowd was able to read the words, "W E L L I N G T O N D E F E A T E D." It is said that at that moment, a thick London fog began to settle in preventing the tower from being visible.

For several hours, a sense of defeat and an anxiousness began to spread across towns and villages throughout England. The Duke of Wellington was their last hope, and that hope had now vanished as he was defeated. Multiple hours into this state of distress shifted as the fog began to lift. As the fog lifted, the rest of the message was now visible: "W E L L I N G T O N D E F E A T E D T H E E N E M Y!"[27] What they had assumed to be the defeat of their last hope was actually their greatest victory. Fog prevented their ability to celebrate and caused them to have a false sense of loss.

HOLE #15

Fog changes our posture when warfare is beginning. My experience is that fog causes the familiar to become confusing. I have missed my turn for the

> Fog changes our posture when warfare is beginning.

very street that I lived on because of the thickness of fog. Fog causes our confidence to become uncertain. Fog causes our strength to become weak. Fog prevents our vision the actual clarity we need. Fog can truly paralyze even the strongest faith-filled Christian, preventing us from adequately preparing for the warfare ahead.

In my life and throughout many ministry moments, I have experienced multiple personal victories, and for that, I am both blessed and still humbled. But sadly, a fog of doubt has often settled in preventing me from celebrating my miracle moments. The therapy that was being provided, allowed the medical personnel to reevaluate my progress and share some good news. After a month of procedures, a surgery and significant therapy teaching me to walk and function again, I finally received my discharge to head home. I was not excited about taking the hardware with me that was still screwed to my head and attached to my body, but I was excited to leave the hospital. The day of my release was when a nurse began to tear up based upon my prognosis. One nurse said, "…you are the eighth person to physically stand up and walk out of this spinal cord unit in the last twenty years. The majority are always wheeled out in what will become their new norm, life attached to a wheelchair. You are so fortunate." While I knew that I was very fortunate, a thick fog had settled over me. That fog covered my mind, my eyes, and to some extent, it even covered my heart. This prevented a clear ability to see what God had done and was continuing to do. As I began to walk outside, I realized then that this was my first day outside in thirty days. The ability to physically walk out of that hospital and experience the great warmth of the California sun for the first time should have brought great joy. Instead, tears filled my eyes based upon the fog that was settling in.

There is a passage in 1 Samuel 30 that I remember stumbling across and finding encouragement in. As I read this chapter over and over, I began to scribble down my own notes of how to overcome the fog when warfare is required. As I read these words, I realized that this would be the message I would want someone to give me in the middle of any crisis. A message of hope, a message of faith, a message that would challenge me to keep fighting. David was King of Israel at this point in history and the men that he was leading were truly the

> Fog can truly paralyze even the strongest faith-filled Christian, preventing us from adequately preparing for the warfare ahead.

best of the best. They were the top leaders and warriors of that time period in history. If we know anything about the journey of King David, we know that he had a reputation as a fierce warrior, a true leader and one who was filled with faith, not with fear. In the first few verses of this chapter, David's posture of victory changes from faith to fear based upon a sense of defeat. 1 Samuel 30:3 says, *"And when David and his men came to the city, they found it burned with fire, and their wives and sons and daughters taken captive."*[28]

> It is my daily reminder that I will never be strengthened by anyone or anything other than my Heavenly Father.

The visual of fire causes me to picture the residue of smoke that filled their camp—similar to a haze of fog that we can experience during our Northern California winter seasons. It was not just a sense of confusion for these veteran warriors, but also a sense of anxiety, and worry that immediately impacted their confidence. Scripture continues by saying that the people who were with David raised their voices and wept until they had no more strength to weep. This position of defeat is what caused even the greatest leaders and warriors to forget Who had walked them through every battle and victory prior to this moment.

If the passage ended there, we would have no hope. In verse six, it concludes by saying, *"...But David strengthened himself in the Lord his God."*[29] In his darkest moment, David was not seeking the comfort of possessions, substances, or even others. He knew that the greatest strength needed would be found through His Lord! It is my daily reminder that I will never be strengthened by anyone or anything other than my Heavenly Father. His strength encourages me. His strength sustains me. His strength covers me. His strength overshadows my crisis. Once we find this kind of strength, we then have the capacity, like David, to receive the action plan that God gives him to overcome his adverse moments.

HOLE #16

The word of encouragement that God gave to David was… *"Pursue, for you shall surely overtake them and without fail recover all."*[30] Some of the greatest warfare moments would be ahead for David and his soldiers and these three areas provide a great foundation for advancement in the midst of our fog moments of this life. God's message of hope for David is what applies to us as well… Pursue, Overtake, and Recover All.

Pursue—David was ordered to pursue the band of men that had caused his greatest pain in that moment. He was charged with the mission of hunting them out. His faith in our Lord supplied him with an inward resource of comfort and energy. This inspired confidence by ordering an immediate pursuit of his enemy, the Amalekites. When the fog sets in with its thick cloud and you can no longer decipher your mission, God is reminding those He's called to return to a godly pursuit. Your pursuit of His original mission will bring about a true inner strength that man cannot measure.

> When the fog sets in with its thick cloud and you can no longer decipher your mission, God is reminding those He's called to return to a godly pursuit.

Again, fog prevents our ability to pursue with confidence. Fog causes any pursuit to become slow. In the midst of adversity, when defeat is the only reasonable emotion, God's challenge to His top leaders of that day was simple... *pursue.* It is not enough to pursue what you have lost, but rather your relationship with Him. Pursue once again with fervor the single mission of your calling and His plans for your life.

The hardest part of the following two months after my hospital discharge was the internal drive to pursue anything. Each day was a repeat of the day before. There was a cycle of daily events that was causing my private fog to become thicker. While I could not find my breakthrough moment in the middle of it, I am now able to see how a breaking point is needed in order to pursue. The ability to pursue the enemy and reclaim all that has been taken happens when we realize the limitations of our enemy.

Growing up in church, it was not uncommon to hear phrases like, "Satan is attacking me," "the enemy is tempting me," among many others. Scripture reminds us that there is an enemy that we are battling. His plan is to *"steal, kill and destroy,"*[31] especially those of us who are followers of Christ. While this is his plan, I have always battled with the balance of how much "credit" he deserves for the crisis moments in my life. Unlike my Heavenly Father, this enemy is not omnipresent. Scripture identifies him as the devil which means "accuser," because he accuses God's people before the throne of God according to Revelation 12. He is known as Satan which means "adversary," because he is the enemy of God. He is called the tempter in Matthew 4 and the murderer and the liar in John 8. He is compared to a lion in 1 Peter and a serpent in Genesis 3. His singular mission in life is to take us out. Though there are spiritual forces at work against us, my Heavenly Father is the only one who is always with me… always with us.

While I could not see this in the middle of my fog moment then, I understand a principle today that has given me the strength to pursue what has been lost. There is an enemy who is targeting me, but I do not have to live defeated based upon my present-day circumstance. What God has promised is far greater than what our enemy has attempted to prevent. And when this is at our foundation, there is no fog that can overshadow our greatest tragedy. My faith in Christ will cause the fog to lift!

Overtake—The next mission assignment that King David received was to "overtake." This is an action word that requires effort and the willingness to surpass or defeat an enemy. In my life, overtaking what has been lost is something that I have waited for God to reveal His timing to me. Unless everything has "lined up," it's not always the easiest to begin. In fact, I now realize that to overtake our enemy requires us to act in moments where there is no time for

> There is an enemy who is targeting me, but I do not have to live defeated based upon my present-day circumstance. What God has promised is far greater than what our enemy has attempted to prevent.

procrastination. A great example of this is found in Genesis with the life of Abraham. When Abraham was given the assignment of sacrificing his son, Isaac, he did not wait till he felt good. Scripture says, *"Early the next morning…"*[32] This means that he did not wait to feel warm and fuzzy inside. He did not ask for another sign from God though he had already heard His voice—something I have regretfully done at times.

King David's mission was to advance toward his goal without delay. They were to overtake the enemy. Oftentimes, it is us who find ourselves overtaken when the fog sets in. Instead of us advancing through it, the fog consumes us, our life, our mission, our vision, our family, our careers, our ministry, and sometimes His will. The word overtake is not to define your state but rather illuminate your mission to recapture what God has called you towards.

There is a strength that each of us need in the middle of our battle, the strength to overtake. This is a declaration of war. This is the attitude in which defeat may no longer be our default posture. Sadly, fog causes us to believe that a true victory will only happen if my prayer is perfectly answered. To overtake means that I am ready to fight, and I know that because I have Christ, I have already won, regardless of how things will end! This is what I prayed in a hospital room by saying, "… if this is what you have for me, then I will be a quadriplegic that worships you." Though the mindset was defeat, it was a warfare declaration to overtake all that the enemy stole from me. I discovered throughout the months that followed, that this overtake spirit would be a sustaining spirit for the mini battles ahead, all of which reaches to this very day.

> The word overtake is not to define your state but rather illuminate your mission to recapture what God has called you towards.

Recover All—Again, King David's mission to pursue and overtake would now lead him to the point of battle. Scripture continues, *"David recovered all that the Amalekites had taken, and David rescued his two wives. Nothing was missing, whether small or great, sons or daughters, spoil or anything that had been taken.*

David brought back all. David also captured all the flocks and herds, and the people drove the livestock before him, and said, 'This is David's spoil.'[33] Not only was every thing returned, but there was also a bounty that David was able to seize from his enemy. It was called, David's spoil. It's hard to imagine how we can shift from a mindset of defeat to a victorious win when we are in the middle of our private battles. Typically, we only see what we have lost, we assume that our life is over, our world is shattered, and we wonder

> **What the enemy intended as harm and grief; the Lord has allowed it to be the blessing with promise for your life. The fog has lifted, and our eyes can readjust to the fact that there is something greater on the horizon than we thought was lost!**

if hope will ever be found again. Our Father's message for those willing to fight and recover all is simple: you will not just have what you lost, there will be an abundance, and that abundance will be above and beyond your loss. What the enemy intended as harm and grief; the Lord has allowed it to be the blessing with promise for your life. The fog has lifted, and our eyes can readjust to the fact that there is something greater on the horizon than we thought was lost!

HOLE #17

I will be the first to admit that the 101 days of intense battle related to an odd golf accident were not faith filled, and warfare positioned. My natural questions were not "how" questions, they were "why" questions. I was not asking "...how do I advance?" "How do I overcome?" "How do I pursue, overtake, and recover all?" My questions were: "Why me?" "Why am I suffering?" "Will this last forever?" "Why is this happening to me?"

As a pastor, I have often had these types of questions posed to me from our church family members in the midst of their pain-filled moments. Some have added to my list of *why* questions by also asking, "...why do bad things happen to good people?" In my life, the *why* based questions I have asked resulted in extended fog induced seasons. Trying to answer the *why* has led me down trails that ended with no hope.

As a Christian, hope that is found in the middle of our crisis moments is the moment we encounter Christ as our Savior. It becomes the moment where faith is discovered in the middle of our suffering. It's the moment where we realize His suffering on the cross at Calvary provides us the victory we need in our current crisis. Jesus suffered so that we could find victory! I am very blessed to declare that I have victory at the end of my physical battle. That victory is found in what doctors described then as a 95 percent recovery from this accident. This included the nearly complete return of range of motion with no paralysis. The 5 percent shortfall of a complete healing is associated with the extensive nerve damage to my left arm. The impact of daily muscle spasms, chronic neck pain, and other side effects is a small price to pay for the ability to walk and run (even though my family believes I drag my foot and mock me often). My physical function no longer requires the usage of the mobility resources my former wheelchairs provided. I am humbled, blessed, and truly grateful that I have been miraculously healed! While this is a true victory of healing, I also celebrate that a private victory took place within my heart and mind. This victory is associated with the outlook and perspective that I carry into every battle that I have encountered since this accident. While I still prepare for the worst and pray for the best, my faith and trust in God to see me through is stronger today and filled with both His grace and His strength. I truly live victorious based upon what God began in my life through this crisis.

> As a Christian, hope that is found in the middle of our crisis moments is the moment we encounter Christ as our Savior.

On Thursday, September 17, 1998, I returned back to the Spinal Cord Unit of Santa Clara Valley Medical Hospital, my first day back since being discharged post-surgery. This trip was not in an ambulance or via helicopter. It was not considered an emergency, but rather the day assigned to see if the halo that had been attached to my body for 101 days could finally be removed. After a series of tests, x-rays, and scans, most of which I had previously encountered, I was left in a room to meet with my neurosurgeon for what would become the final time. I remember him walking in and stating that everything looked great, and that it was time to remove the halo.

Unlike the time of my halo hardware installation, the removal of a halo did not include any anesthetic. A fancy drill was brought into the room and a technician began to unscrew each bolt. The sensation of a screw turning and the realization that it was happening slightly below the brain that is processing everything I'm hearing and feeling was surreal. The momentary pressure with an almost instantaneous relief after the first screw was removed was a very odd feeling. When the fourth and final screw was removed and the hardware began to be removed, there was a sense of suspense in that room.

I am not certain if I was expecting my neck to instantly collapse due to the weight of my head, but I do remember holding as still as possible for as long as I could. As my doctor returned to my examination room, I believe we both felt as if we were meeting for the first time. It was the first time that I was able to greet him by physically standing up with no hardware attached and reaching out my hand to shake his while expressing my personal gratitude.

Before I departed the hospital, there was one final piece of business that my doctor wanted to discuss with me. He said, "Abe, as you know, the halo and brace is a very expensive medical device that many third-world countries cannot afford. Because of this, we ask all patients if they are willing to donate this hardware so that someone less fortunate can benefit." So much had happened in the past 101 days. My world had been flipped upside down (literally and symbolically). As a pastor, I knew that this would form the lifetime message that God would use through me, and all I heard was a doctor asking me to give away the greatest (and most expensive sermon illustration I had ever experienced). Whether it was selfish or not is still to be determined, but I declined and said, "…having that halo displayed in my office will be the greatest testimony of what God has done. Thank you, but I'm keeping it!" And with those words, I was discharged with the assignment of physical therapy and a few checkups to follow throughout the first year alone.

HOLE #18

No one can convince me that the lessons experienced during this season of my life have not strengthened me, even though it was the most physically painful experience that I have encountered in my life (to date). This journey in many cases solidified my faith and reestablished my foundation of trust in Him during dark and trying periods. It also has challenged me to ask and answer the question of what God was attempting to teach me during these times.

As always, it is much easier to process that question decades later as opposed to the moment of great impact. In fact, one church member visited me early on in my hospital stay and thought it would be the perfect time to ask the question, "…what do you think God is wanting to teach you in this hospital based upon your condition?" I will admit that my answer was very sharp and rude but was the perfect summary of what I felt in the moment. In that setting, I replied with "Patience… God has attached me to this bed so that I can't physically beat you." As a result, he left. Though his question was poorly timed, it is a fair question and one that is worth exploring.

Decades later, I see how God was using and still uses this pivotal turning point in my life as a filter for everything related to faith in Him. One of the many lessons I have experienced since is a greater sense of empathy for those alone in a hospital battling their faith to believe in healing. During my hospitalization, I was introduced to a teenager from my city who was involved in a gang-related drive-by shooting. He was paralyzed from the waist down and confined to a wheelchair. I was asked to pray for him by my pastor while I was in the hospital just several doors away from my room. To be standing at his bedside while wearing my halo was one of the hardest things I had done during my hospitalization. I was in my own crisis of faith and didn't believe I was the best person to speak faith into another person's crisis. But that moment provided a great bond. Upon both of our discharges from the hospital, he would begin attending our church with his family. None of that would have ever been a possibility had it not been for the shared experience of surgeries, wheelchairs, therapy, and much more. The difference between us, however, was that he was confined to a wheelchair. Praying with this student in the hospital was hard. Praying with him multiple times after was a great privilege. Hearing him say that his only prayer was to walk across the stage for his high school graduation broke my heart. Initially, all I could see was a kid in a wheelchair hoping to walk again. What he could see in front of him was a picture of what he was then and what he could be based upon my miracle. For nearly a year, we prayed this same prayer, almost every week. One of the greatest joys was standing on the sidelines of my old high school football field during his graduation. Watching him be wheeled to the stage that day was emotional. But nothing prepared me for the moment that he stood up, and with the help of arm and leg braces, walked the length of the stage having just graduated high school. With tears in my eyes (and tears in the entire crowd present), I quietly said to God, "…if all of this was for this student, I do believe there were other ways to get my attention and send me to his hospital." God's reply to my selfish state was, "You may have gone to visit, but you would never be able to relate like he needed." Today, I count it one of my greatest privileges to visit those waiting through their hospital stays. This is not because I am a pastor, but because I have been on the other side of that equation and was encouraged and strengthened by those who did the same for me.

It would be this very accident that would shape my understanding and value of family. I have been blessed with one of the best, but the crisis revealed a whole new depth of love. To have a mom quit her job and move into my apartment as a primary caregiver for nearly three months is humbling and was a true blessing. To have a dad offer his resignation to his company after nearly thirty years of service, only to have it rejected and then granted as much medical leave as was needed to make the nine-hour drive between our two states is priceless. To have a teenage sister sacrifice her summer to sit bored in an apartment for endless weeks still astonishes me. None of it should be a shock based upon my amazing family, but I remain grateful for their willingness to stand with me in a season in which I could not stand.

It would be this very accident that would remind me of the need to still laugh, especially at myself. It would be the sight of a McDonald's outside my first hospital window that caused me to crave their "Quarter Pounder," something I have only done once in my life. It would be the first time that I sneezed with a halo on, that an entire room would freeze. They were unaware of what was happening, and I was afraid that the pressure would cause the screws to shoot out of my head with the same force as a missile being fired from a battleship. It would be something so painful in the moment that would cause mostly everyone else to at least smile privately without me seeing it. To laugh is an expression of joy, something that God began to restore long after my accident.

It would be this very accident that I was reminded of the value of a friend. On the one-year anniversary, nearly my entire original group of golfer friends gathered to finish the round that we never completed that day. To be together was a joy. To be able to walk was a blessing (as I also promised my wife that I would never again use a golf cart on that course). To be able to have a birdie on that hole (two strokes, one better than the average or par) would have been a miracle, but I missed. The difference is that I now have the perfect excuses as to why I am so bad at a sport that I still enjoy (this book now serves as a recorded document as to why I just lost my last round). What makes it richer are those that I choose to play with for the investment of time over a five-hour round of golf. There truly is nothing greater than close friends!

It would be this very accident that would define my future family. I knew that Anna was God's gift to me and for my life, but a crisis like this prior to wedding vows being exchanged shifted my perspective. As a pastor performing many wedding ceremonies, I have led couples through the traditional phrases, "… for better, for worse, for richer, for poorer, in sickness and in health…" It's one thing to say it, but very rarely do couples have a chance to witness it in action before the words are ever stated. During this 101-day period, Anna drove a minimum of sixty to100 miles roundtrip to be by my side as a source of strength and comfort. It revealed the true gift that God had brought into my life, something that I still am grateful for to this day! Our marriage and family are not defined upon a past accident, but rather the godly foundation of these vows long before they were publicly declared to each other on July 31, 1999 (thirteen months after my accident).

It would be this very accident that would give me a future confidence of trust and true faith in my Heavenly Father as my Provider. To be transferred to Valley Medical Hospital was something considered out of my insurance network. This would result in additional fees beyond their normal charges. But to land on that roof on June 8, 1998, allowed me to be treated by a neurosurgeon who "ranked" in the top ten in the nation. Watching the way that God miraculously provided for my medical expenses is nothing short of another series of miracles. I had quoted Philippians 4:19, but now I was, and I still am living it, *"And my God will supply every need of yours according to his riches in glory in Christ Jesus."*[34] It has reshaped my ability to trust in my Lord for everything I need.

Many of my medical records still show that I am a quadriplegic. This has provided me with great moments of fun as I have laid perfectly still in examination rooms and then rolled off the table as doctors and nurses have entered. It still shocks me that I can scare them even though I walked in. It was somewhere in the middle of my journey that I heard a minister friend share something intending to be an encouragement to the questions surrounding "why are these things happening?" He said, "God will not trust you with more than you can handle." I remember being encouraged with that at first and then reflecting upon the thought, "I wish God did not trust me so much!"

There is not a day that has passed since, that I have not experienced some level of pain that dates back to my accident. For some, that would be depressing. For me, it's a reminder of God's promise. And it now becomes my prayer for all of those who find themselves in the middle of a crisis, near the end of a crisis, or even those who have no idea that they are beginning a crisis.

I pray that you discover these truths that I am still learning and experiencing. He has never left me or forsaken me. He still walks with me through every valley moment as well as the mountain top encounters. He is with me, in the same manner as He was with each of those in scripture that we read about and find greater faith because of. He has rescued me from a pit, set my feet firmly on this foundation and given me a hope like I have never previously experienced.

I now pray that this book becomes a personal encouragement to you in the middle of your own faith-trying moment. Me yelling "FORE!" throughout this book is no longer a warning cry or a cautionary scream. Scripture reminds us that "... *Weeping may endure for a night, But joy comes in the morning.*"[35] This book is now a reminder that a crisis can either paralyze you or strengthen you, but a crisis is never the end. Any crisis can define you, or you can define your crisis as you put into practice these godly principles that lead the way through your own darkness and discover HIS magnificent light.

About the Author

Rev. Abe Daniel has been in pastoral ministry since graduating High School in 1994. Since age eighteen, he has served the greater Church in youth, music, and administrative ministries as a staff pastor, a denominational director with the Assemblies of God, and Senior Pastor of Trinity Life Center in Sacramento, CA.

Abe and his wife Anna have been married since July 1999 and met while attending Bethany College (University) in the mid-1990s. Abe majored in Church Leadership/General Ministries at Bethany and completed a Master of Arts degree in Global Ministry Design from Moody Bible Institute in 2020. He has begun a Doctoral program through Southeastern University that will conclude in 2025. Anna majored in Social Science while at Bethany, received her Master of Arts in Education in 2008, and has taught English and History in public and private middle schools. Abe and Anna have three sons, Abraham, Andrew, and Mathew.

Prior to his senior pastoral role, Abe served as the District Student Ministries Director for the Assemblies of God for nearly eight years, during which he provided leadership development for 440 churches throughout Northern California and Nevada. It was during this season that he began a unique ministry called Pathway. Within five years, Abe launched seventy-two graduates of Bible colleges, universities, and internships into full-time ministry. Pathway has since morphed into an educational platform based out of Trinity Life Center. Today, Pathway assists leaders with their ministerial requirements, having impacted all fifty states, eleven additional countries, and over 1000 leaders since 2019.

Abe considers it a great honor to have traveled extensively domestically and globally ministering in churches, conferences, camps, and conventions. For more information, please visit: www.abedaniel.com.

Endnotes

1   https://www.dictionary.com/browse/defining-moment?s=t
2   http://bleacherreport.com/articles/540759-50-greatest-golf-quotes-of-all-time
3   http://www.scottishgolfhistory.org/origin-of-golf-terms/fore/
4   John 16:33 (ESV)
5   John 16:33 (MSG)
6   Wiersbe, Warren, The Wiersbe Bible Commentary: New Testament (Colorado Springs, Co: David C. Cook, 2007), 293
7   Psalm 23:4 (ESV)
8   Proverbs 17:17 (ESV)
9   1 Peter 4:12 (ESV)
10   2 Corinthians 12:9 (ESV)
11   http://bleacherreport.com/articles/540759-50-greatest-golf-quotes-of-all-time
12   http://www.dictionary.com/browse/despair
13   Genesis 39:2-4 (ESV)
14   http://www.dictionary.com/browse/diagnosis?s=t
15   http://www.dictionary.com/browse/prognosis?s=t
16   Genesis 39:21-23 (ESV)
17   Psalm 119:11 (ESV)
18   Thomas, R. L. (1998). *New American Standard Hebrew-Aramaic and Greek dictionaries : updated edition.* Anaheim: Foundation Publications, Inc.
19   http://bleacherreport.com/articles/540759-50-greatest-golf-quotes-of-all-time
20   Psalm 40:2 (ESV)
21   https://www.songfacts.com/facts/darlene-zschech/shout-to-the-lord
22   http://enrichmentjournal.ag.org/200101/0101_118_prayer_changes.cfm
23   Hebrews 4:14-16 (ESV)
24   http://bleacherreport.com/articles/540759-50-greatest-golf-quotes-of-all-time
25   https://www.mayoclinic.org/symptoms/blood-clots/basics/causes/sym-20050850
26   https://www.history.com/topics/british-history/battle-of-waterloo

[27] https://www.sermoncentral.com/sermon-illustrations/79416/wellington-defeated-by-milo-velebir

[28] 1 Samuel 30:3 (ESV)

[29] 1 Samuel 30:6 (ESV)

[30] 1 Samuel 30:8b (NKJV)

[31] John 10:10 (ESV)

[32] Genesis 22:3 (NIV)

[33] 1 Samuel 30:18-20 (ESV)

[34] Philippians 4:19 (ESV)

[35] Psalm 30:5b (NKJV)

Lightning Source UK Ltd.
Milton Keynes UK
UKHW011011070223
416609UK00006B/1589